On Being a Jew

a Jew

A Reform Perspective

Published by
Holy Blossom Temple
Toronto, Ontario, Canada

CANADIAN CATALOGUING IN PUBLICATION DATA

Marmur, Dow
    On being a Jew : a Reform perspective

Includes bibliographical references and index.
ISBN 0-9698469-0-8

    1. Reform Judaism. 2. Judaism—Essence, genius, nature.
I. Holy Blossom Temple (Toronto, Ont.). II. Title.

BM565.M27   1994   296.8'346   C94-900464-2
© 1994 by Rabbi Dow Marmur

Edited by
Judy Nyman and Ruth Chernia

Published by
Holy Blossom Temple
1950 Bathurst Street
Toronto, Ontario M5P 3K9 Canada

Design and Typesetting by
Nyman Ink

Cover by
Marla Tenby

Printed in Canada

This book is dedicated to the Presidents of Holy Blossom Temple during the first 10 years of my tenure — "bosses" who became friends:

Myer Brody (1983 – 1984)
Gordon Wolfe (1985 – 1986)
Fred Zemans (1987 – 1988)
Richard Krelstein (1989 – 1990)
Nancy Ruth (1991 – 1992)
Diana Goodman (1993 –)

Contents

Foreword

The congregation is privileged to honour Rabbi Dow Marmur's first decade of service to Holy Blossom Temple with the publication of this book.

The themes expressed reflect the depth of spirituality and commitment to the ideals of Judaism we have come to associate with him.

During the past 10 years, he has engaged us and challenged us on a wide range of important issues and we look forward to many more years as beneficiaries of his wisdom and guidance.

Together, may we go from strength to strength.

— *Diana Goodman, President*

We gratefully acknowledge the participation of the following congregants whose generosity helped make this publication possible.

Patrons

Mr. & Mrs. George A. Cohon Mr. Robert Lantos
Dr. & Mrs. Burnett Thall

Sponsors

Mr. Mark S. Anshan &
  Dr. Brenda J. Spiegler
Dr. & Mrs. Lawrence Ballon
Mr. & Mrs. Thomas Beck
Mr. Earl & Mrs. Ann
  Bederman
Dr. & Mrs. Barnet Berris
Mr. & Mrs. Warren Biback
Mr. & Mrs. Lawrence
  Bloomberg
Mr. & Mrs. Zelik Bocknek

Mrs. Rae Bookman
Dr. & Mrs. Barry Borden
Mr. & Mrs. Harvey Borden
Mr. & Mrs. Edward Borins
Judge Stephen & Dr. Elaine
  Borins
Mr. & Mrs. Myer Brody
Judge Reuben & Mrs. Elizabeth
  Bromstein
Dr. & Mrs. Elie Cass
Mr. & Mrs. Charles S. Chaplin

Mrs. Henrietta Chesnie
Dr. & Mrs. Louis Cole
Mr. & Mrs. Hilliard Conway
Dr. & Mrs. Peter Dan
Mr. & Mrs. David Dennis
Mr. & Mrs. Elliott Eisen
Mr. & Mrs. Larry Enkin
Mr. & Mrs. Morris Finsten
Mr. & Mrs. Lloyd Fogler
Mr. & Mrs. Alan Garfinkel
Mrs. Rose Garfinkel
Mr. & Mrs. John A. Geller
Mr. & Mrs. Irving Gerstein
Dr. & Mrs. Bernard Goldman
Mr. & Mrs. Marvin B. Goodman
Mr. & Mrs. Gary Griesdorf
Dr. & Mrs. Brian Hands
Mr. Elliott Jacobson &
  Ms Judy Malkin
Mr. & Mrs. Ivan Jaye
Dr. & Mrs. Jerome Kazdan
Ethel & Ron Kellen
Dr. & Mrs. Laurence Klotz
Mr. & Mrs. Richard Krelstein
Mr. & Mrs. Joseph Kronick
Mr. & Mrs. Morris Latchman
Mr. & Mrs. Donald Loeb
Beverley & Joseph Lokash
Mr. & Mrs. Richard Lorie
Mrs. Queene Luxenberg
Mrs. Renee Lyons
Professor & Mrs. Harold Minden
Harley Mintz & Judy Nyman
Mr. & Mrs. David Mirvish
Mr. & Mrs. Ed Mirvish
Mr. & Mrs. Saleh Mukamal
Mr. Allan Offman

Mr. & Mrs. Martin Offman
Mr. & Mrs. Harry Pachter
Mr. & Mrs. Harry Pearl
Mr. & Mrs. Yitz Penciner
Dr. Sheila Pollock
Mr. & Mrs. Gary S. Posen
Mr. & Mrs. Theodore Rachlin
Mr. David Raitblat & Dr. Reva
  Gerstein
Dr. Barry Rosen & Ms Beth
  Goldstein
Dr. & Mrs. Robert Ruderman
Mr. & Mrs. Sam Ruth
Mr. & Mrs. Robert Salsberg
Dr. Sandra & Mr. David Sandler
Mr. & Mrs. Leo Schacter
Mr. & Mrs. Paul Schnier
Mr. & Mrs. Brian Schnurr
Mr. S. Harlan Schonfeld &
  Ms Ruth Mesbur
Dr. & Mrs. Saul Sidlofsky
Mr. Bob & Mrs. Sheila Smolkin
Mr. & Mrs. Gerald Slan
Paul & Carol Slavens
Mrs. Isadore Smith
Mr. Bert & Mrs. Barbara Stitt
Mr. & Mrs. Martin Storm
Dr. & Mrs. Marvin Tile
Dr. & Mrs. Alan Track
Paul & Iris Vanek
Dr. & Mrs. Jean-Victor
  Wittenberg
Mr. & Mrs. Gordon Wolfe
Mrs. Rose Wolfe
Professor & Mrs. Frederick
  Zemans
Dr. & Mrs. Bernard Zucker

We also express our thanks to those individuals who contributed through all other sources.

Acknowledgements

I am most grateful to all who have made this book possible, and would like to add my personal thanks to the contributors listed in Diana Goodman's Foreword. I am deeply touched by their support and generosity.

Without Diana Goodman (President of the Temple), Gary S. Posen (Executive Director) and Hugh Furneaux (who helped us turn a nebulous idea into a reality), this project would not have been possible. It is my privilege to thank them publicly for all their help.

My secretary Hilary Kay and the editors Judy Nyman and Ruth Chernia have devoted many hours of hard work in putting this volume together. My gratitude to them is boundless.

Finally, I would like to express my appreciation to the publications and organizations for permission to reprint pieces that previously appeared under their auspices. Apart from editorial changes in an effort to create a measure of uniformity in this book, the texts are substantially the same. Though sources are acknowledged in each chapter, I would like to take this opportunity to thank:

ARZA, the Association of Reform Zionists of America, and its Executive Director Rabbi Ammiel Hirsch (chapter 10).

Compass, the Jesuit journal (chapter 20).

The Institute for Cultural Research, Tunbridge Wells, England (chapter 1).

The Law Society of Upper Canada (chapter 6).

New York University Press (chapter 15).

Manna, the publication of the Sternberg Centre for Judaism, London, England, and its editor Rabbi Tony Bayfield (chapters 5, 16 and 23).

The Reform Synagogues of Great Britain (chapter 3).

Sh'ma, the journal of Jewish responsibility (chapter 13).

The Toronto Journal of Theology (chapter 19).

Viewpoints, the Canadian-Jewish periodical, which appears as a supplement to the *Canadian Jewish News*, and its editor Bill Abrams. Eight chapters of this book are taken from *Viewpoints*: 2, 8, 9, 11, 14, 17, 18 and 24.

All errors and omissions are, of course, mine and mine only. I apologize for them in advance.

— *D.M.*

Introduction
From Survival to Continuity

Chapter 22 of Genesis tells how the patriarch Abraham bound Isaac on Mount Moriah in response to what he understood to be God's command to sacrifice his only son. In this way, he demonstrated his obedience to God and his trust that his son would be spared. Much of what being a Jew is about is linked to this story. Hence the countless interpretations and legends around it.

One such legend has it that when Abraham and Isaac were on their way up the mountain, Satan — in Jewish tradition not so much the personification of evil as the leader of the heavenly opposition — intercepted them and urged Abraham not to carry out his mission. Satan's argument was clever. He said: If you sacrifice your only son, this will be the end of the Jewish people, for you have no other recognized offspring and now, surely, your wife is too old to have more children. He added: Having prayed so hard for this son, don't give him up now! But Abraham replied: Survival is God's business; my task is to do God's will. And father and son continued on their way.

Because Abraham obeyed God, and ignored Satan's clever intervention, there are Jews in the world today. We have survived and, through us and our offspring, Abraham's line has continued. Being a Jew is, first and foremost, being a descendant of Abraham and Sarah.

Synagogues are the most effective institutions in the Diaspora, for they make it possible for these descendants to become the disciples of Moses. It is in synagogues that Torah is taught and practised. It has been my privilege to serve three of them, two in Britain and, since August 1983, Holy Blossom Temple in Toronto.

When I came to Canada, the buzzword in the Jewish world was still "survival." Elie Wiesel — the foremost spokesperson of the generation of Holocaust survivors whose writings have inspired chapter 15 in this collection — described Isaac as the survivor par excellence. Emil Fackenheim — who came to articulate post-Holocaust Jewish theology and is frequently referred to in this volume — had formulated the so-called 614th commandment: Survive, for you must not give Hitler a posthumous victory! It had become an article of faith of a whole generation of Jews still traumatized by the Holocaust. They wanted nothing to do with Abraham the obedient believer in God; their hero was Isaac the survivor.

Fackenheim's formula, despite its religious purpose, had become particularly popular among secular Jews, for it enabled them to be Jewish without practising Judaism. They could disobey, even rage against, God and yet affirm their Jewishness. To be described as disciples of Satan would only have added to their fury. For, as long as they wanted to survive as Jews — so they chose to understand Fackenheim — they were doing God's work, not Satan's, even if they didn't believe in either.

The new, 614th, commandment, heard from between the chimneys of the gas chambers, had for many annulled the other 613. Jews now came to believe that they could be passionate about Jewish survival, and live as authentic Jews, without knowing the purpose of Judaism or caring much about the future. All that mattered to them was that the enemy must not have the last word; that Jews must not be defeated, despite the pain and the wounds.

That this approach should have been in conflict with Orthodox Judaism, with its emphasis on obedience to the 613 commandments and its rejection of every form of addition and innovation, is obvious. But so pervasive was this secularism that it had also invaded our own Reform ranks. As a result, our theology became hardly distinguishable from sociology, and our avowed commitment to prophetic Judaism manifested itself as little else than a taste for Jewish politics. God was written out of the script, or so circumscribed by fashionable terms as to be impossible to identify.

In this secular climate, those who insisted that they were religious liberals — with a universalist emphasis on human responsibility to care for the survival of the whole world as God's domain, not only for the Jews — were often ridiculed. Religious liberalism was so intimidated that it no longer dared speak of spirituality or articulate belief; if Reform meant anything at all to followers and foes alike, it was as a euphemism for non-observance, a synonym for secularism and an antonym to Orthodoxy. Much that the reader will find in the pages that follow challenges this approach. It offers a vision of Reform Judaism that is neither Orthodox — for it advocates *mitzvah*, commandment, not *halachah*, law — nor secular, for it repeatedly affirms the God of Abraham, Isaac and Jacob.

Israel's political shift to the right exploited the doctrine of survivalism. Deliberately or otherwise, the political leaders of the Jewish state made us set aside many cherished Jewish values in the name of loyalty to Israel and solidarity with the Jewish people. These sentiments were so strong that even the fiasco of the 1982 war in Lebanon inhibited us from articulating a realistic, balanced Jewish perspective. Many of us believed that whatever was done, was done for the sake of Jewish survival. Therefore it was, by definition, sacred and beyond moral scrutiny.

We had confused the voice of Satan with the command of God. We could disguise our disregard for the 613 commandments and claim fierce loyalty to the State of Israel in the name of survival. Israel became identified with the 614th commandment that replaced all the others. This book, while affirming the centrality of the land of Israel, offers a very different view.

Things have changed in the course of the last decade. To start with, the political map of Israel has been altered. Our loyalty to the Jewish state need no longer be in conflict with Jewish values. On the contrary. Peace with neighbours — even when it is risky, and when they are nasty — and justice for all — even when it is painful — have once again been brought to the fore of the Jewish agenda. Progress towards peace with the Palestinians and other Arabs has helped us realize that the quest for our own survival is intimately bound up with our concern for the survival and well-being of others, even of our enemies.

We also understand that when we do God's will by acting according to the teaching of God's Torah, we will deserve to live on, as Isaac did — even when we appear to be in peril, as he was. Even ardent secularists have learnt that survivalism as a doctrine may be comforting to Jews traumatized by the Holocaust, but it is meaningless to their children. They want to know *why* they should survive before they accept *that* they should survive. Hence the renewed emphasis on religious life despite all secular temptations. Religious liberalism has meaning again; Reform Judaism is not just form but content. This book tries to articulate that content.

The wholesome shift in Israeli politics has led to a welcome and long overdue shift in the Diaspora's vocabulary. We now speak less of *survival* and more of *continuity*. The difference between the two terms is substantive. For, whereas our quest for survival forced us to be primarily *re*active to threats from outside, the stress on continuity prompts us to be *pro*active, to formulate Judaism positively in the light of the opportunities within and the challenges without. I hope that this volume testifies to the shift.

Immediately after the Second World War, the shock of the Holocaust — coupled with the dramatic access to power through sovereignty in Israel, and full emancipation in much of the Diaspora — turned Reform Jews into adolescents who had just been given freedom and who, therefore, wanted to live in the here and now, rather than care about a nebulous future. Survival was seen in the present only. Half a century later, we have gained a perspective on the memory of the Holocaust and on the experience of freedom: We have grown up as Jews. Hence our reaffirmation of God and of tradition. Though still reluctant to commit ourselves fully, we are beginning to face the message of the new era. We have come of age, and, as adults, we recognize that the present is meaningless unless it points to a future; that survival is futile unless it assures us of continuity; that Jews cannot live in this world as if neither God nor the rest of humanity mattered.

My reservations about survivalism and the politics that go with it are not new. They were part of the agenda I brought with me to Holy Blossom Temple. The year before I arrived, I published a book called *Beyond Survival* in which I argued my case. Several chapters that follow reiterate and develop this argument.

But, what I have to say now may not seem as controversial as it did a decade ago. Then, we still liked to think of ourselves as a hounded minority, children of poor immigrants and Holocaust survivors, exposed to the mercy of the gentile world, on temporary vacation from blatant anti-Semitism. We are now ready to think again and recognize that the threat to our existence does not come from the foe outside, but from the failure within; not from the danger of persecution that threatens our survival, but from a failure of nerve and a failure of faith that puts continuity at risk; not from the threat in the present, but from the fear of the future. What is required from us is not defensive survivalism, manifest in bombastic slogans, as Satan would want it, but affirmation of Judaism as the basis for solid continuity — in obedience to God. We are purging ourselves of secularism. I would like this book to be a contribution to the process.

Judaism

Strictly speaking, chapter 1 does not belong in this volume, for it was published before I came to Holy Blossom Temple. I have, nevertheless, included it because it echoes ideas in my first book, *Beyond Survival*, and thus provides a starting point for what this collection is trying to say.

Chapter 2 is a summary of my third book, *The Star of Return*, published in 1991. The ideas contained in both works have been carried forward, and, I hope, developed in the following two chapters.

Preparing this volume has made me aware of how much of an insider/outsider I am, in North America in general, and within the Reform community in particular. Most essays imply it, but chapter 5 states it specifically.

The two last chapters in this section, devoted to Jewish law and its implications for Reform Judaism today, further attest to a point of view not normally heard in the circles of North American Reform. I hope, however, that it will be acceptable to Canadian readers.

Among them, these seven essays offer a thumbnail sketch of my understanding of contemporary Judaism and, therefore, form the basis for the book as a whole. That's why they have been placed first, even though some readers may find them heavy going. I can only hope that their perseverance will be rewarded.

1

The God of My Parents — the God of My Children

The Amida, the central prayer in the Jewish liturgy, includes the words, "Our God and God of our Fathers, the God of Abraham, the God of Isaac and the God of Jacob." Does this mean, commentators have asked, that Judaism implies more than one God; that "our God" differs from "the God of our Fathers?" Surely, to Judaism's strict monotheism, that would be an absurd assumption! And yet, where the Hebrew language could tolerate a phrase like, "the God of Abraham, Isaac and Jacob," the text deliberately repeats "God" before mentioning each of the three patriarchs. Why?

The traditional answer is that, although God is the same, the individual has to find God for himself or herself, and, therefore, is bound to perceive God differently. God does not change, but since each person's perception is different, individual and very limited, one can, at best, only fathom the reality that is God. Thus God — who is always the same — is different in the perception of Abraham, Isaac, Jacob and all the prophets, sages, scholars and ordinary folk who came after them. Tradition is the sum of these experiences and, yet, also incomplete: it beckons us to add our own.

Jewish tradition, is both "our God" and "the God of our Fathers"; it is "the God of Abraham" and "the God of Isaac" and "the God of

Originally published as, "The God of My Fathers — the God of My Children" in *The Nature of Religious Man: Tradition and Experience*, ed. D. B. Fry (London: The Octagon Press, 1982), 53–64.

Jacob"; and it is God as perceived by prophets and priests in the Bible, by the rabbis of the Talmud, by philosophers from Philo to Buber, by the codifiers and the preachers through the ages, by mystics and rationalists, by fundamentalists and liberals. It is the God of patriarchs and matriarchs; it is the God of our parents as well as our God. Jewish tradition is the sum of these in a composite and complex picture that we describe as Torah.

Originally, the term Torah was used to denote the Pentateuch only, but, in time, it came to describe all of Jewish tradition. As a rabbi, I speak as an exponent of that 3,000-and-more-year-old tradition.

I cannot ever do it full justice. I can, however, look at it from my particular perspective, which is something like this: In certain epochs in Jewish history, for example, in the Middle Ages, exponents of Judaism preferred to look backward instead of looking forward. For valid historic reasons, they sought to chart the past in as much detail as possible. They assumed that to know what the God of our Fathers wanted of them and who God was for them, would almost automatically tell us who our God is for us and what God wants of us. A popular expression of this kind of religiosity is reflected in the phrase, "What was good enough for my parents is good enough for me." A deep reverence and piety for the past follows this, a reverence that, for all its nobility, masks a crippling insecurity and leads to a staid, well-ordered and legalistic way of life.

The most effective way for earlier generations to break out of this spiritual straitjacket was through mysticism. By its nature — and often despite outward "respectability" — mysticism was daring and experimental. Jewish mysticism almost invariably retained a loyalty to, and a reverence for, the past. Yet it also enabled its adherents to find "our God," not only in terms of "the God of our Fathers."

Much in modernist Judaism builds on this tradition. However, under the influence of modernity, Jewish movements that emerged after the emancipation of the Jews in the eighteenth and nineteenth centuries were more interested in stressing "our God" and more prone to criticize, even denounce, the kind of religiosity that hides behind the pietistic phrase, "the God of our Fathers." These movements were no longer satisfied with the maxim, "What was good enough for my parents is good enough for me." Instead, their slogan was, "What is good enough for my children is good enough for me." In contrast to mediaeval Judaism, modern Judaism became future-oriented. This does not mean Jewish modernists ignored or minimized the past. They just viewed it differently and refused to be bound by it.

As a Reform rabbi, I speak from this modernist perspective. For me, the past is not, as it is for an Orthodox Jew, the final guide and arbiter. Rather, it is a source of inspiration, the stuff out of which my own religious life can be shaped. The past may be my first source of religious guidance, but it is not my only one.

Pointing to the most ancient of Jewish symbols, the seven-branched candlestick, let me try to offer seven reasons for this modern Judaism.

One: A Source of Wisdom

The first reason why Judaism matters to Jews and fascinates non-Jews is because it carries a store of wisdom. Of course, other religions also contain wisdom, but the style and content of Jewish teaching is, naturally, different and distinct. It has influenced the daughter religions of Christianity and Islam, and is a strong component in our western culture. Jewish tradition describes this wisdom as Torah, to which I have already referred. Torah manifests itself in two ways: as education — a system of holy study; and as law — a system of codes and practices.

Jewish tradition teaches that Torah is the revealed will of God. Whether you take it literally, which is the Orthodox approach, or metaphorically, which is the modernist view, it means that to study the sources of Judaism is to perceive more correctly and more comprehensively what God wants of us. To my parents this would have meant that every word of Scripture, and of the oral tradition that developed around it (recorded in the Talmud, in the codes, in Jewish philosophy and literature) had to be taken literally; for my children, and, indeed, for me, this means that the Torah is a human response to God's call. But for all, the study of Torah is a holy pursuit. It takes precedence over most other religious activities, even prayer, and, as such, is absolutely central to Jewish religious life. To study, you do not even need an *a priori* commitment, just an open mind and a sense of awe and wonder, which is the beginning of faith. Judaism is so convinced about the intrinsic power of the message that it believes that once you study it diligently, you are bound to want to live by its precepts. Conversely, the lack of faith and the lack of piety are often seen as signs of ignorance. A rabbinic saying has it that "an ignorant person cannot be pious."

Moreover, it must always be understood that the purpose of study is right action, the carrying out of God's will as revealed in Scripture and commentaries. Therefore, Torah is never *just* education but always *also* law, rules and regulations designed to govern every detail of our lives. It is in practice that the commitment is measured, not in dogmatic statements or articles of faith. The principle applies whether you are a fundamentalist or a modernist. The former is bound to try to accept everything; he or she may be weak enough to escape the law but would never try to change it, because to change would imply a challenge to the authenticity of tradition and the veracity of the word of God. If you seek to modify Jewish law, you become almost automatically a modernist.

In this respect, then, I differ from my parents. On the basis of what I know about biblical criticism and historic development, I see tradition, not as immutable, but as a record of how previous generations responded to revelation, to the call of God. Because of what I know, I feel compelled to offer my own response: to learn from them and to follow them whenever their response is true for me, but to modify, change and innovate when it is not. This is what makes me a modernist.

But, whether fundamentalist or modernist, adherence to Torah is basic. The Pentateuch is read in the Synagogue on Sabbaths and festivals. Members of the congregation are called upon to recite a benediction before each reading. The central theme of the benediction is praising God for having chosen us from all peoples and given us the Torah. "Chosenness," then, is not favouritism, arbitrarily bestowed, but a vocation to study and to practise.

Two: A Sense of History

To be Jewish means, to almost every Jew, to see oneself as a link in a long chain. To understand the present and to respond to its challenges means to know what has gone before and why. Let me try to explain it in terms of a paradigm recorded in Genesis 32.

After many years abroad, the biblical Jacob returns to his home country. On the way, he hears that his brother Esau, whom he had left in haste and with much unfinished business, is coming towards him with 400 men. Jacob is confused. Is this to be an encounter between brothers, and are the 400 men an impressive guard of honour? Or is this to be a battle, and are the 400 men an army to settle an old score? Jacob makes preparations. He sends a delegation to appease Esau with gifts and he divides his camp in two. He spends the night before the decisive encounter alone. During the night, a mysterious being wrestles with him, but as dawn is breaking and the attacker cannot prevail, Jacob extracts a blessing: he shall no longer be called Jacob but Israel. So Jacob walks away from the struggle with a dislocated hip — and with a blessing.

The book of Genesis, which tells this story, does not inform us who the mysterious being was. There are many speculations and interpretations. The medieval Jewish commentator, Rashi, summarizing rabbinic tradition, identifies him as "the guardian angel of Esau."[1] Bearing in mind that in that tradition Jacob represents the Jew and Esau the gentile, Rashi's interpretation becomes significant: Jacob the Jew, the spirit of Hebraism, wrestles with the spirit of the surrounding gentile world. By surviving the struggle, Jacob *becomes* Israel. He is maimed, but also blessed. Seen in this light, the biblical story in its rabbinic interpretation becomes a paradigm for Jewish existence: Israel is the result of the struggle between the spirit of Hebraism and the surrounding civilization. It is a painful and beneficial encounter. Only in this way can Jacob become Israel.

Jewish history can be viewed as a succession of encounters of this kind. Each is a risk *and* an opportunity. The risk is annihilation; the opportunity is renewal and rebirth. In our time, the former is symbolized by Auschwitz, the latter by the existence of the State of Israel.

To recognize this drama and try to discern its purpose, is to perceive something of the essence of Judaism: that is, to view chosenness not as favouritism, but as a peculiar obligation. Part of that obligation expresses itself in the need to honour the memory of the martyrs of our people. To know what happened to Jews in the Hitler period has become a kind of religious duty; to prevent its recurrence has become another, and greater, one.

It is in this context that it may be possible to understand the Jewish preoccupation with the Jewish state. I know it is fashionable to accuse Jews of being racist, imperialist and militarist, and to identify us with every possible anti-symbol. But I believe, sadly, this is the price we must pay for being conscious of history as part of our religious heritage. For Jews, the State of Israel is nothing more than a chance, perhaps the only chance, to remain Jews and to ensure that never again will six million of us be led as lambs to the slaughter. It is possible that in the eyes of our non-Jewish neighbours we may seem somewhat hysterical. But I hope our friends will understand our reason; that they will appreciate the sense of history that evokes this response.

In modern Jewish theology, survival has become a religious category. In the words of Emil Fackenheim, only by surviving as Jews can we prevent Hitler from having a posthumous victory. The State of Israel is the vehicle of that quest of survival. Only through it can Jews find purpose, despite Auschwitz. More recently, the stress on survival has been augmented by an affirmation of continuity; there are signs of less emphasis on the present and more on a vision of the future.

Three: An Ability to Feel Pain

The talent for remembering our own pain, and trying to feel the pain of others, is life-affirming, not life-denying. The commitment to try to alleviate pain helps us not only to find purpose but also joy in life. Judaism is a happy religion; its solemnity is never less than joyous. In this respect, it contrasts sharply with the secularism of our time that, for all its clamour for "paradise now," appears gloomy and dull. What is so characteristic of Jewish humour — to be able to laugh with one eye and cry with the other — is a true reflection of the Jewish attitude to life.

Four: Community

Our affirmation of life and need to care express themselves in the seemingly ordinary: in the family, the congregation and the community at large. Community is yet another link between parents and children.

The joy of having survived and being alive prompts us to share this joy with others. We do so by celebrating holy events in the life of individuals and in the history of our people. This helps us cement relationships and relive the past. Many of our rituals and ceremonies are linked to the sense of community. They offer a framework of security in the midst of a perplexing and hostile world. For non-Jews, this seems at times bizarre and exclusive, and evokes a mixture of envy and hostility on which anti-Semitism thrives. Much of Jewish life takes place in the family and in the extended family we call our congregation or community. The rabbi acts as teacher and catalyst, not as priest. He or she is also the person who often seeks to find a way of linking "our God" with "the God of our Fathers." The community offers the milieu that makes such a bridge possible.

Five: God

A congregation is a *kehilla kedosha,* a holy congregation. Belonging is not only a matter of survival, but a question of spiritual integration, of holiness. The Jew who wishes to be part of the Jewish community identifies with the quest for spiritual integration or holiness. It is the experience of Judaism that God cannot be found on a remote island but is revealed in the midst of the people; Scripture insists that the whole Israelite community was present at Sinai. God is not an *a priori* category, a philosophical abstraction with which one has to start one's religious quest. Instead, God is to be sought in the company of like-minded seekers. To belong to a community does not mean that you start with certainties, but that you have a desire to look for them. That is why so many seemingly irreligious Jews belong to congregations. Through membership in the community, I am exposed to what Peter Berger, the sociologist, calls "signals of transcendence," intimations of what it means to be with God.[2] Through the community, I may be able to experience God even when I do not understand. That is why, in this list of the seven branches of Judaism, God is not mentioned first, but only after Torah, history, pain and community.

This does not mean, of course, that belief in God is unimportant in Jewish tradition. What must be understood, however, is that a philosophical conception of God is not a prerequisite for being a Jew. You start by sharing the wisdom, the history, the pain and the community. Through these, you may come to an experience of God. And, as I said, although God is One and Unique and always the same, we perceive God differently. That perception, however, becomes pale and, at times, even misleading if we try to confine it to a definition. God, Jewish philosophers have taught, can only be described by negative attributes: we can say what God *is not*, but it is impossible to say what, or who, God actually *is*.

Martin Buber reflected much of this in his writings: God can only be addressed; God cannot be expressed; we can speak *to* God but not *about* God. Buber has shown how we can receive intimations of God — Berger's signals of transcendence — through interpersonal relationships. Through an I-thou relationship, I can move towards a relationship with the Eternal Thou. By contrast, philosophy and abstract theology can only perceive God as an object, as an "it," thus becoming a barrier rather than an aid to faith. Jewish tradition bears out Buber's idea of God. Never does it demand a confession of faith, an adherence to dogmas. We are entitled to perceive God differently, because we are not expected to define our perception.

We cannot express God, only address God, and we feel more confident to do so when we are with like-minded people in the midst of a worshipping congregation. That is why the community is there, not only to teach the wisdom and the history and share the pain, but also to help us to pray together. Prayer reflects tradition and yet stresses immediacy; through it, we can celebrate our special relationship with God. Chosenness, in this context, resembles the relationship of lovers. The biblical prophets used the image of marital love as a metaphor for the relationship between God and Israel. The Song of Songs was included in the biblical canon as the perfect allegory of that relationship. The Christian distinction between *eros* and *agape* — human love and divine love — is, therefore, unknown in Judaism. The commandments "Love the Lord your God" (Deuteronomy 6:5) and "Love your neighbour as yourself" (Leviticus 19:18) use the same Hebrew word, *v'ahavta.*

Despite the apparent exclusiveness, everybody can share the relationship exemplified in the dual commandment to love. For God is the God of all humanity. Scripture begins with Adam, the first man, not with Abraham, the first Jew. In this universal scheme of things, Israel has a special task: it is to be the catalyst, whose concerns are the concerns of the whole world. Redemption is not reserved for the Jewish people, but must come to all humanity. The nations of the world will deserve it by being true to their ancestral faiths — in the same way as Jews must be true to their religion, Judaism.

Six: Testimony

Our real aim is to testify to the presence of God. The Jews see themselves as having the duty to testify to the power and reality of God in the world. Through the study of Scripture, tradition and history, I can establish a link with the past, a line of communication with the God of my parents. Through the experience of pain, I must affirm life. One manifestation of this affirmation is the emphasis on human relationships: the family and the community. Such relationships point to the source of all love, God. Through our collective experience of pain, we are made to love humanity and to love God. The problem of theodicy is resolved in the determination to alleviate misery. In this way, we come to testify to Job's affirmation, "though He slay me yet will I trust in Him" (Job 13:15). This testimony is particulary poignant in our generation when Auschwitz survivors could praise God and speak of God's power and goodness, despite all that befell them.

To be a Jew, then, is something of a heroic act. We are not Jews because it is comfortable but, whether it is or not, we discharge our responsibility to God by affirming our Judaism. Being Jewish in the face of persecution and assimilation is a religious act. It brings us beyond the dichotomy of universalism versus particularism. Chosenness is not self-centred or smug, but a messianic obligation. Isaiah's suffering servant is the Jewish people itself, a line of exegesis suggests. Israel's history reflects God's plan for the world. Israel seeks to share its insights and experience with others, not to convert, but to show, through autobiography, rather than theology, that God is and that God must be adored and obeyed, even when God appears remote and angry.

Seven: Hope

All this becomes possible only through the Jewish propensity for hope, another theme to which we will return later. Protestant theologian, Jurgen Moltmann, in his *Theology of Hope,* showed that Judaism is founded on the idea of covenant. God says to the people: Here are the commandments; if you observe them I will carry out My part of the agreement and take you to the Promised Land.[3] By accepting my responsibilities and my obligations as a Jew, by living my Judaism, I am stating my conviction that God will keep the other part of the "bargain" and bring about a better tomorrow. Hope becomes a function of my religious life. I don't just wait for the Messiah to come, but I actually walk towards him.

This message of hope is of particular relevance in our age of gloom. That is the only way I can understand Isaiah's injunction to Israel to be "a light unto the nations" (Isaiah 51:4), a light in this age of darkness. The sense of personal privilege of being a Jew is mingled with my universalist sense of obligation to testify to the message of Judaism. My religious commitment enriches my life and encourages me to share the wealth through the act of testimony. Imbued with a measure of Jewish wisdom, Jewish history, Jewish pain and Jewish community, I testify to God. I hope in God's promise that tomorrow need not bring disaster, because obedience to God will merit benevolent divine intervention. It also, finally, dissolves the apparent dichotomy between the God of my parents and the God of my children. The messianic vision of Malachi has it that on "the great day of the Lord," when God's intervention will finally become visible to all, "God shall turn the heart of the fathers to the children, and the heart of the children to their fathers" (Malachi 4:5–6).

Notes

1 Rashi on Genesis 32:24

2 Peter L. Berger, *A Rumour of Angels* (Harmsworth, Middlesex, England: Penguin Books, 1971).

3 Jurgen Moltmann, *Theology of Hope* (New York: Harper & Row: 1967).

2

Judaism After the Holocaust

A quarter of a century ago, the leading Jewish theological journal, *Judaism,* published a symposium entitled, "Jewish Values in the Post-Holocaust Future."[1] One participant was Emil Fackenheim, at the time, a professor of philosophy at the University of Toronto. His contribution to the symposium is best remembered for the startling assertion that Auschwitz, in all its horror and tragedy, has, almost like a second Sinai, given us an additional commandment. Sometimes called the 11th commandment, after the biblical 10; sometimes the 614th, after the rabbinic 613: the commandment is to survive and, thus, deprive Hitler of a posthumous victory. The Nazis wanted to exterminate the Jews; by its continued existence, the Jewish people defeats the Nazis' monstrous purpose.

Fackenheim's formula has had an enormous impact on contemporary Jewish thought, but, as will become evident, I do not necessarily share his views.

The title of the book I published in England in 1982, *Beyond Survival,*[2] is an implied challenge to Fackenheim's commandment. The book argues that survival may have been the appropriate message for the generation that witnessed the Holocaust, but it is not sufficient for their children and grandchildren. For them, mere survival is not enough; they want to know the purpose of survival. And that has to be formulated in positive terms, not as an act of defiance against Hitler's determination to destroy us.

Reprinted from *Viewpoints* 21:1 (1992).

From the outset, I questioned Fackenheim's formula for post-Holocaust Judaism, and I continue to do so today. My 1991 book, *The Star of Return*,[3] tries to carry on the quest begun in *Beyond Survival*. Although Fackenheim is only mentioned by name five times, the book owes much to him, whether it agrees with him or not.

It agrees with him about the centrality of Israel in contemporary Jewish life, but it disagrees on *why* Israel is central. Fackenheim's stress on survival brings him to affirm the State of Israel as the surest guarantor that Hitler will not get his posthumous victory. The theme of my book stresses the centrality of Israel, not because it guarantees Jewish survival but because it defines Jewish purpose. By inference, this also guarantees survival yet goes beyond it. This leads us to different conclusions and different politics.

The starting point of *The Star of Return* is the understanding of Judaism as a triangle, the sides of which are faith, people and land. Had Judaism been only a faith, like Christianity, we would have been only the disciples of Moses *rabbenu*, our teacher, through whom the Torah became our possession. But we are also the descendants of Abraham *avinu*, our father (and, I hasten to add, Sarah, our mother). The faith of Abraham and our other patriarchs and matriarchs — from whom we originate — and the faith of Moses — the teacher of our people — was grounded in a covenant with God. The subject of that covenant was the land of Israel. God said to Israel: If you obey My commands, I will bring you to the Promised Land. Since biblical times, therefore, we must speak — in one breath — of Israel as faith, people and land, for the covenant links them and thus defines our spiritual heritage.

Those who disagree with this understanding of the nature of Judaism say that, for most of our history, the vast majority of Jews have resided outside the land of Israel and yet fully lived their Judaism. Therefore, they conclude, it is inappropriate to regard land as central; it is the text of the covenant and its history that stand in the centre of Israel.

My contention is the opposite. Look how strong the attachment to the land of Israel has been! Even after millennia of dispersion, we still fix our gaze on it when we pray, and we mark time according to the seasons there, no matter in which country we live. The land has been so important that it has been an integral part of Judaism, even when it was physically inaccessible. Even the most pious and observant Diaspora Jews believe they could only live their Judaism to the full in the land of Israel. Their need for the land was so strong that they linked its repossession to messianic times.

True, it has always been very difficult — and after the Holocaust, which totally destabilized Jewish life, it became even more so — to position ourselves in a balanced fashion within the triangle of faith, people and land. Therefore, many have tended to confine themselves to one side or another. Thus, pre-Holocaust, classical Reform tended to define Judaism primarily in terms of faith — symmetrical to Christian faith, and with little allegiance to the people or the land of Israel. Similarly, secularists have understood Judaism primarily as people — an approach well suited to a country such as Canada, where ethnicity is much stronger than religiosity. Finally, many Israelis, and some non-Israeli Zionists, centre their Judaism on the quest for land. Each of these approaches is partially right, but each is also totally wrong. To understand Judaism in terms of one of its components, while ignoring the others, distorts its true nature. To separate Judaism into its alleged components is to dismember it.

If, for much of its history, Judaism has existed, even flourished, without access to land, it is because the faith and the people have been so strong that Jews could imagine the land without being there. What is nonsense in geometry — a two-sided triangle — has been a Jewish reality for some 2,000 years.

Modernity has challenged all that. The European Enlightenment, which reached Jews at different times depending on when and where they emerged from the ghetto, devastated their Jewish faith. Even those who continued to affirm Judaism — as classical Reform did — as a counterpart to Christian faith could usually only muster lukewarm allegiance. And this often became progressively weaker with successive generations, just as in Christianity. Simultaneously, modern anti-Semitism, the devastating by-product of emancipation, weakened the Jewish people, culminating in the Holocaust when a third of all Jews were physically exterminated and the rest were deeply shattered. Because of the dual onslaught of Enlightenment and anti-Semitism, Jews could no longer maintain the triangle and, consequently, Judaism was in danger.

The simultaneous erosion from within — in the form of loss of faith — and attack from without — in the form of persecution — was too much to withstand. When Hitler was finally defeated, Judaism was so weakened that Hitler may have been close to his posthumous victory. One dare not speculate what would have happened to Judaism had there not been a Zionist movement to point camp survivors towards Israel.

Judaism was saved when the remnants of the people of Israel returned to the land of Israel. Of course, the process began with the early Zionists more than half a century before the establishment of the State of Israel in 1948. But it was only Jewish sovereignty, three years after the end of the Holocaust, that made possible the renewal of Judaism that we are now witnessing. The return to the land of Israel has led to a revival of the faith of Israel and the restoration of the people of Israel. It has affected every movement and reached every country where Jews live by enabling them to locate their spiritual heritage in the triangle. The revival of religious faith and the renewal of the Jewish people are the direct results of the return to the land of our ancestors.

The restoration of Judaism in our time can best be described in terms of a paradigm shift. A characteristic feature of a new paradigm is that it is really not that new at all. It is merely a novel restatement of old truths that, for one reason or another, were left out or ignored in the old paradigm. Unlike political revolutionaries, scientific innovators are not usually iconoclasts, but classicists: men and women who find new meanings in old truths. This is the model that I wish to apply in order to try to understand the revival and the renewal following the return. It explains the shift from a Judaism centred on survival — the ghetto — to a Judaism centred on purpose — the land.

However, although most Jews are supporters of Israel and even speak of its centrality, the nature of that support must be questioned for at least two reasons.

First, most Jews living outside Israel do not believe they should even contemplate living in Israel. As far as they are concerned, the Jewish state is there for hapless refugees who have nowhere else to go. That is why American Jews — which means most non-Israeli Jews

— do not even see themselves as living in the Diaspora. When they speak of the centrality of Israel, they do not mean that, because of its existence, their own Jewish focus has in any way shifted. Though they are mouthing the language of the new paradigm, they are living by the principles of the old. *Aliyah*, emigration to Israel, is not an option for most Jews living in the free world; it is only a necessity for those who have nowhere else to go. Zionist ideology has led to Jewish philanthropy, and contemporary Judaism has become subject to market forces.

Second, and more significant, Jewish life is still organized on the principle that its greatest threat is anti-Semitism. Of course, there is much anti-Semitism about, and, of course, it has to be fought resolutely. But anti-Semitism does not threaten the core of Jewish existence today, although it may threaten the existence of individual Jews and some Jewish communities. And anti-Semitism has become less threatening precisely because Israel exists. The new paradigm makes the old arguments — and the old defences — obsolete, although many neurotically still hold on to them. While refusing to contemplate *aliyah* and the opportunity to live in the sovereign Jewish state where there is no anti-Semitism, we live as if anti-Semitism threatens us with extinction. It is an attitude that made sense before Israel existed; it does not make sense today.

Neither does it make sense to regard the existence of Israel as under the constant threat of anti-Semitism, and to view every critic of Israeli government policies as a Jew-hater. A fundamental mistake of Diaspora Jewry is to defend Israel on the grounds that it is a victim. It is nothing of the kind, and thank God for that! Those who are prepared to take the step beyond survival and move towards purpose become less concerned with strategy — fighting enemies — and more with the content of Judaism — being witnesses to the presence of God in history. A growing number of Jews today want to know how to lead Jewish lives more than how to fight anti-Semitism because they know that living as Jews will, by definition, protect them against extinction.

It is worth observing in this context that secular Jews are usually much more preoccupied with anti-Semitism than religious Jews. Fighting anti-Semitism is the only Judaism secularists know, and in their secular self-contradiction, they celebrate Fackenheim for having elevated their neurosis to a divine commandment. They may also have a personal interest in combatting anti-Semitism as it so often impedes their efforts to be accepted by the non-Jewish world. Jews of every religious denomination who practise their Judaism are much more concerned to do God's will than to fight enemies. They know that, to the extent that they succeed in obeying God, they will also survive as Jews.

In this light, let us look again at our understanding of the Holocaust. The conventional view of contemporary Jewish history sees the Holocaust as a prelude to the creation of the State of Israel. This is the myth of Holocaust and redemption. We all recoil from implying that the Holocaust is the price the Jewish people had to pay for Israel. We know that even the triumph of statehood could not have warranted the tragedy that preceded it. But most of us, nevertheless, connect the two events. When United Jewish Appeal missions stop in Auschwitz on their way to Israel and the March of the Living takes Jewish children to Poland for *Yom Ha'shoah*, Holocaust Memorial Day, and then on to Israel for *Yom Ha'atsmaut*, Israel Independence Day, the message is that the Holocaust is a prelude to Israel and that the two must be understood together.

By contrast, I believe that the Holocaust is the last and most gruesome manifestation of the old paradigm, the one that left Jews to the mercy of others. I view Israel as the celebration of the new paradigm, the one that enables Jews to have as much say in their own destiny as any other free people. The conventional view regards Israel as a potential victim and equates anti-Zionism with the old anti-Semitism. My approach celebrates Israel as the victor and views Zionism as the liberation movement of the Jewish people. This means the Holocaust and Israel belong to different categories.

I base this contention on the fact that the new paradigm — modern Zionism that created Israel — was born 50 years before Hitler came to power. However, then its proponents were no more than a few conspirators. Only after the Holocaust, and even more so after the Six Day War, has it become clear — but, alas, still not to the majority — that the old paradigm is dead and the return to the land, as formulated by Zionism, is the new paradigm.

The difference between the two approaches is fundamental. To view the Holocaust as a prelude to Israel leads to a very different perception of the Jewish state than to see Israel as an old-new beginning. The former sees Israel as a refuge for persecuted Jews and an avenue of escape in case life becomes difficult in the Diaspora. The latter sees the land of Israel as a place where the Jewish people, at last, can testify to the Jewish faith — just as the Bible has charged us to do, and as we have been unable to do because we have been persecuted. It is the difference between a Judaism based on survival and a Judaism based on purpose and continuity.

Purpose points to solidarity. When we stress survival above all else, we see no reason to try to "mend the world." Instead, we argue that, since the world has not been prepared to protect us, we have to look after ourselves, whether the world likes it or not. It is a manifestation of a ghetto mentality, for it decides moral issues based on if they are good or bad for the Jews, not whether they are right or wrong by universal standards. Instead of making us act to make a good impression on non-Jews, which is the criterion of the old, the new paradigm demands that we do the right thing in the eyes of God, according to the standards laid down in the Torah.

When we stress solidarity, we reformulate the biblical doctrine that we must be kind to strangers and support the helpless because we were strangers in the land of Egypt. Because we have been the victims of evil, we are called upon to fight evil wherever we find it. The Jewish state can never be less than a refuge for all Jews, but it cannot be only that. It must also be an exponent of Judaism, and thus a force for justice and goodness in the world. The return of the people to the land is validated by the faith.

David Hartman — a Canadian, now living in Israel, who has enriched post-Holocaust Jewish thought — said (in a lecture delivered in Toronto some time ago) that when he moved to Israel, he became much more of a universalist than when he was a rabbi in Montreal. Living in the old paradigm ghettoizes us by forcing us to fight for our survival, while ignoring our purpose. Living in the new paradigm liberates us to do God's work and lets survival take care of itself.

Notes

1 *Judaism* 16:3 (Summer 1967).

2 *Beyond Survival* (London: Darton Longman & Todd, 1982).

3 *The Star of Return* (New York: Greenwood Press, 1991).

3

From Civility to Piety: An Agenda for Postmodern Judaism

Long before I came to Toronto, I learned to appreciate the writings of Rabbi W. Gunther Plaut, one of my illustrious predecessors at Holy Blossom Temple, who has become a dear friend. I was particularly impressed by a survey of the history of Reform Judaism I heard him deliver at a convention of the World Union for Progressive Judaism. His paper was subsequently published.[1] I refer to it in each of the three books I have produced in the last 10 years.[2]

Plaut divides the history of Reform Judaism into different phases, each answering a specific question. According to him, the early founders of Reform Judaism sought, first, to answer the question, *Ma yomru ha'avot?* 'What do our ancestors, or rather, what does tradition say?' In this phase, "the past was explored so that it might shed light on the present."[3] This was the time when Reform Judaism, with the help of scholarly insights and rational arguments, wanted to establish its authenticity in the eyes of Jewish history.

The second phase sought to address the question, *Ma yomru hagoyim?* 'What does the non-Jewish world say?' Plaut writes that

Originally delivered as the Inaugural Jubilee Lecture, under the auspices of the Reform Synagogues of Great Britain, at Manchester University, England, on May 21, 1992, and subsequently published as a pamphlet by that organization.

this "was a period in which the demands, the ideologies and the opportunities of the environment were dominant and when, at the same time, a distinct (though unconscious) shift away from the new Orthodox East European immigrants was observable." This was the time when the exponents of Reform Judaism were most anxious to make the "right" impression on the non-Jewish world. They did so partly by imitating it and partly by presenting Judaism in a "favourable" light, in the vain hope of combatting ignorance and anti-Semitism.

The third phase, which started about the time the Nazis came to power in Germany, was characterized by the question, *Ma yomru habanim?* 'What will the children say?' "Now," writes Plaut, "no longer was the issue, 'How do we adjust to the impact of the environment?' Now it was, 'How can we save our people and secure a future for our children?' Israel was one answer, and another was Jewish education, which came fully into its own." Having sought to justify itself to the Jewish past and the less-than-Jewish present, Reform now tried to address its future, and the precarious future of the Jewish people.

The fourth phase sought to answer the question, *Ma yomru chayyay?* 'What will my own life say?' From the 1960s onward, we tried to meet the needs of people interested in their own spiritual journey and personal fulfilment and, therefore, less concerned with the first three phases of Reform Judaism. This quest for the therapeutic attracted many rabbis of my generation. They thought they could teach better Torah in the consulting room than in the school or the pulpit.

Of course, when a new phase emerged the previous phases did not disappear from our world; they co-existed. That is why, today, the four most salient characteristics of Reform Judaism have been shaped by the four phases: (1) our struggle with tradition; (2) our involvement with the non-Jewish world, which, of course, also means non-Jewish culture; (3) our emphasis on education and other means of Jewish survival; and (4) our pastoral pre-occupation with the needs of individuals.

You have only to survey the activities and interests of contemporary rabbis to find each of these elements strongly represented: their dialogue with Jewish law; their interest in presenting Judaism to non-Jews; their motivation to teach; and their training in counselling skills.

Although this essay is not only about Reform Judaism, I have chosen to begin it in this way to suggest that Reform is especially hospitable to what is normally known as civil religion, the most potent manifestation of modernity in the Jewish community. Although civil religion affects all religious movements in Judaism, other than the ultra-Orthodox, it is particularly dominant in our own circles. It is, therefore, right and proper that Reform Jews should pay more attention to it than others. By defining our present situation in the context of civil religion, we may better understand Jewish modernity, its tremendous opportunities and its ominous shortcomings.

Jewish civil religion has been impressively documented by Jonathan Woocher.[4]

Woocher identifies seven tenets of "the civil Jewish faith."[5] Together, they form the creed of most contemporary Jews. They are (1) the unity of the Jewish people, (2) mutual responsibility, (3) Jewish survival in a threatening world, (4) the centrality of the State of Israel, (5) the enduring value of Jewish tradition, (6) *tzedakah*: philanthropy and social justice and (7) Americanness as a virtue.

It is not too difficult to match at least three of Plaut's four phases with Woocher's seven tenets. Thus Plaut's first phase — striving to justify Reform in terms of the Jewish past — is reflected in what Woocher calls "the enduring value of Jewish tradition." Plaut's second phase — seeking justification in the eyes of the gentiles — is reflected in the tenets Woocher calls *tzedakah* and Americanness; and Plaut's third phase, which stresses survival, is reflected in the rest of Woocher's list: the unity of the Jewish people; mutual responsibility; survival in a threatening world; and the centrality of the State of Israel.

If Plaut's fourth phase has no counterpart in Woocher, it is because Jewish civil religion is primarily concerned with the collective. The fourth phase of Reform Judaism, on the other hand, reflects its strong and characteristic emphasis on individualism. The answer to the question, What does my life say? is nowadays being sought not in community, but in "lifestyle," which is often the antithesis of community, and thus outside the realm of civil religion.[6] Individualism is a manifestation of "the culture of narcissism," whereas civil religion is concerned with the life of the community.[7]

But apart from its communal, often high-minded nature, Jewish civil religion is too much civil and too little religion to satisfy spiritual needs. Although nothing in it contradicts normative Judaism, there is much in Judaism that it does not address. Above all, civil religion is silent about God. It is strong on identity but weak on holiness. To quote Woocher again:

> Theology, except at the most rudimentary formulaic level (where even atheists and agnostics can be accepting of God-language as metaphorical) is inherently divisive in contemporary Jewish life. By remaining silent on the nature or role of God in human life and Jewish destiny, civil Judaism avoids antagonizing any of these Jews.[8]

This brings Woocher to this conclusion: "Civil Judaism is thus clearly a religion of horizontal transcendence, of covenantal responsibility, stretched across space and time. But its lack of theological content undermines an active affirmation of vertical transcendence."[9] Quoting the historian and sociologist Daniel Elazar, Woocher suggests that civil religion seeks to recreate the Judaism of the Sadducees which "places at the centre of its world not Torah, but the Jewish people, and makes the maintenance and expression of Jewish peoplehood its primary religious obligation."[10]

This means that our Pharisaic heritage, which has shaped normative Judaism, is being squandered: "American Jewish civil religion departs from the Pharisaic-rabbinic mode not only in its refusal to embrace *halachah* as a binding norm, but by explicitly shifting the primary locus of Jewish meaning back into the public realm."[11] It legitimatizes, according to Woocher, "a way of being Jewish and a program of Jewish activity within which the role of the synagogue and the rabbinate — the life of study, prayer and ritual observance — are no longer primary."[12]

To the extent that the synagogue remains important, it is because it reflects the tenets of civil religion. The Kol Nidre service, for example, has become an excellent opportunity to raise money for

Jewish causes from "the captive audience," rather than an occasion to ask God to forgive the sins of the worshipping congregation. In civil religion, philanthropy comes before theology and solidarity with Israel before fidelity to God.

Much of this is the result of the failure of modernity. However, before I attempt a critique, let me state the obvious: Modernity, particularly in its technological manifestation, is here to stay. We are not likely to return to premodern technology. Even those who say they want to do so, tend to change their minds rapidly when they are sick and need the resources of nuclear medicine or laser surgery. And modernity has been good for humanity in general and the Jews in particular. Only with the new opportunities this century has provided could Jews establish themselves in the world as we have done, despite the Holocaust. Similarly, the existence and security of the State of Israel depend on modern technology. The Jewish population of Israel will never outnumber its enemies, nor will it ever have more money than they have. It is only the Jews' ability to adapt to modernity in a way the Arabs have not, that has made Jewish sovereignty possible in our time.

Civil religion is a product of this adaptation. We have assimilated to the American way of life, not because we want to deny our Jewishness, but because we want to live and thrive as Jews. This means that civil religion, though insufficient for our spiritual life, is beneficial for our physical well-being and we must affirm it, even when we cannot embrace it. Only fundamentalist extremists seek to reject it, but even they are less than consistent about it.

We, on the other hand, do not wish to go backward, but forward into what I have hinted at as the postmodern world. Though we affirm modernity, we are very critical of it. Let me offer four samples of the kind of criticism of modernity that is being heard today: one each from philosophy, politics, sociology and theology.

(1) Charles Taylor is a leading philosophic writer of our time. In 1991, he gave the Canadian Broadcasting Corporation's Massey Lectures. Their title says it all: *The Malaise of Modernity*.[13] The three malaises with which he deals are, first, breaking loose from older moral horizons brought

about by individualism, second, rationality that makes us calculate the most economic application of means to a given end and regard maximum efficiency as the measure of success and, third, loss of freedom that results from applying the previous two criteria.

(2) Vaclav Havel, the remarkable President of the Czech Republic, opened his speech to the world Economic Forum in Davos, Switzerland, in February, 1992 by declaring that the upheavals in his country and elsewhere mark the end of modernity. As reported in the *New York Times*, March 1, 1992, he said: "In the deepest sense, the end of Communism has brought a major era in human history to an end. It has brought an end, not just to the 19th and 20th centuries, but to the modern age as a whole."

(3) Zygmunt Bauman has called his important book *Modernity and the Holocaust*.[14] It is a persuasive illustration of the connection between the mass destruction of Jews and modernist thinking — philosophic, technological, bureaucratic. It points to Taylor's second malaise of modernity. The Holocaust was the victim of an ideology, Nazism. And all ideologies are evil, which is what Havel was speaking about in Davos.

(4) Eugene Borowitz, the prime exponent of liberal Judaism in our time, calls a chapter in his latest book "Modernity — the Betrayer." In the first paragraph of that chapter he writes:

> Suddenly our society's accepted, unbounded faith in human accomplishment began to seem ludicrous. Each day's telecast brought into our homes numbing evidence that, along with its many benefits, modernity has also created new and intense forms of human misery. The disillusionment touches us in ways as local as the threat of drugs, violence or the loss of meaning, and as global as pollution, terrorism or nuclear destruction.[15]

Borowitz wants to affirm the world of technology and much of the civil religion of American Jewry. But he also wants to go beyond it: hence the subtitle of his book—*A Theology for the Postmodern Jew.* To do so, he seeks to combine the traditional Jewish idea of covenant with the philosophy of Martin Buber. Buber maintained that reality only takes place when partners in dialogue affirm each other. He argued that this is not only true of human encounters, but also when we encounter God. With the help of Buber, Borowitz seeks to move us beyond civil religion, from horizontal to vertical transcendence, from civility to piety.

Although I speak from the tradition of Reform Judaism, my concerns are with Judaism as a whole. In that vein, I would like to reflect on an important aspect of the writings of Rabbi Joseph Soloveitchik, the great contemporary exponent of mainstream Orthodoxy.[16]

The basis of Borowitz's postmodern theology is the account of the covenant in the Book of Exodus. The starting point of Soloveitchik's thought is the twice-told story of creation in the opening chapters of Genesis. Modernity, as manifest in the so-called higher criticism of the Bible, has taught us that the reason we have two creation stories is because the texts, as we now have them in Scripture, have been compiled from earlier, no-longer-extant, documents. As an Orthodox Jew, Soloveitchik, naturally, repudiates the documentary hypothesis. Instead, he insists that both stories are needed to convey the two dimensions of human existence and, therefore, both contain the authentic words of the living God. Whether or not his exegesis is correct, his conclusions are interesting and relevant. They may help us along the path we wish to take, for they offer a view of humanity that speaks to us.

Even if Soloveitchik's account is defective biblical scholarship, it is brilliant *midrash* when he points out how Adam, the prototype for all humanity, is depicted differently in the two biblical accounts of creation. In the first, Adam is strong and sovereign:

> And God created man (that is Adam) in His image, in the image of God He created Him; male and female He created them. God blessed them and God said to them, "Be fertile and increase, fill the earth and master it; and

rule the fish of the sea, the birds of the sky, and all the living things that creep on earth." (Genesis 1:27–28)

In the second creation story, Adam is weak and vulnerable, created "from the dust of the earth," (Genesis 2:7). Here, Adam is anything but self-sufficient; he depends on God's continuous intervention.

The two stories, according to Soloveitchik, reflect the two dimensions of humanity. The first tells of the self-sufficient master of technology, the hero who made modernity possible; the second describes the fragile human being. Only the two accounts together can tell us who we really are. In the words of a Yiddish proverb, "A person is, simultaneously, stronger than iron and weaker than straw." To live as human beings in the postmodern age is to understand ourselves as Jewish tradition, according to Soloveitchik, understood the first man.

By contrast, the modern age celebrates only Adam the first and neglects Adam the second. The philosopher Taylor, the politician/playwright Havel, the sociologist Bauman and the theologian Borowitz each say so from his own vantage point. If we are to learn from them, and countless other teachers of our time, we can, at best, only partly affirm modernity. In significant respects we must reject it. Therefore, even when we do not oppose civil religion, we cannot settle for it.

Plaut's first four stages of Reform Judaism and the seven tenets of Woocher's civil religion belong to the world of Adam the first. They assume that human beings, equipped with political opportunities and technical skills, are really in control. They forget that this is only one side of humanity and the other, the weak and vulnerable Adam, is being suppressed in the process. That is why, incidentally, Adam the first has such an enormous need for psychotherapy. The consulting rooms are filled with strong and successful men and women who repeatedly ask "What does my life mean to me?" Had Adam the first, to use the psychotherapeutic imagery of Carl-Gustav Jung, been in closer touch with Adam the second — his "shadow" — by being not only civil but also pious, there would be much less need for therapy. The couch can never be a substitute for the pew.

Unlike the flight to premodernity, which seeks to negate Adam the first, the postmodern quest attempts to restore the balance by reaffirming Adam the second, without negating Adam the first. Hence our renewed stress on spirituality and our recognition that piety has to be added to civility, if we are to remain integrated human beings and authentic Jews. It is not a matter of Adam the first — self-reliance and technology — or Adam the second — spirituality and prayer — but both. However, in view of the present imbalance, it is the spirituality and the prayer that need particular emphasis.

Soloveitchik believes that the integration of the two Adams can only be done through *halachah*, Jewish law.[17] I would like to argue otherwise by suggesting that the postmodern era is also the post-halachic era. But unlike the modernist exponents of civil religion, those who seek to move beyond modernity are not anti-halachic. That does not mean, however, that they wish to return to the long premodern, halachic epoch in Jewish history.

Borowitz repeatedly affirms the centrality of Jewish observance, yet finds it impossible to accept the strictures and impositions of Jewish law. He repudiates the premodern notion of a coercive deity and an obedient humanity — the notion that led to the rejection of transcendental religion in the modern world. He argues in favour of a mutually sustaining partnership between God and the people, and sees no place in Jewish life today for a law that commands Jews from "on high" and forces us into obedience governed by the rule of a fundamentally immutable law:

> With so many Jews only willing to accept *halachah* as guidance, I am convinced that we have come to an end of the period when Jewish living could still be disciplined by rabbinic *halachah*. By contrast, I believe that the relational theory of revelation generates the possibility of creating its own pattern of giving form to Jewish life — its own halachic structure.[18]

I prefer to make the distinction between *halachah*, the discipline of a binding Jewish law that is no longer tenable, and *mitzvah*, the notion of commandment to which every authentic Jew must respond voluntarily. I no longer believe it is possible to retain the halachic structure in the postmodern world. The way in which liberal Jews still try to struggle with Jewish law may be intellectually stimulating, but I doubt if it has practical relevance.

One reason I changed my mind was because I now can observe the American Conservative movement. It has valiantly tried to give meaning to Jewish law in our time. However, when confronted with practical issues, such as the ordination of women — a supreme challenge to *halachah* — it either has had to break with halachic practice or revert to Orthodox *halachah*. The result has been very little progress in postmodern *halachah* and a very serious split within the Conservative movement.

Let me offer two other reasons for my change of mind. First, Jewish law, by its nature, is collectivist. Jewish existence in this postmodern era is, on the other hand, individualist. Even when we believe that Jewish observance is important, we are only likely to accept it on a voluntary, autonomous basis: as an imperative we impose on ourselves and that, probably, only sporadically and inconsistently. And even when Taylor expresses misgivings about modern individualism, he knows that, at best, it can only be tamed, not eradicated.

Even when we seek community, as I believe we must to live authentically as Jews, we will only do so voluntarily. Rabbis and lay leaders have only as much authority as the members of the community grant them. If the clergy and the *machers*, 'activists,' seek to exceed that authority, they will soon be ignored or dismissed. The era of the autocratic rabbi or community leader has long passed.

Even the Jewish state is not governed by *halachah*. To the extent that political expediency has given the Orthodox rabbinate in Israel authority in matters of Jewish status, it has turned Israel into a medieval society. For the most part, however, the State of Israel follows an amalgam of British, French and Turkish law, not the Talmud and the codes. And it is this legal system that has made Israel the modern democracy of which we are so justifiably proud. Had the *halachah* governed Israeli society, it is very unlikely that the state would have survived. At best, it would have been a relic ruled by the *Neturei Karta*, the ultra-Orthodox sect.

Which brings me to the second reason why I think *halachah* is no longer operative in the postmodern era of Jewish history: Jewish law is no longer the binding force of Jewish life; the State of Israel — the same State that is not governed by *halachah* — fulfils that function. While *halachah* has become an ominously divisive force in Jewish life — not only between Orthodoxy and its alternatives, but even more ferociously between various groups within Orthodoxy — the security and prosperity of Israel are the forces that bind most Jews to each other and to Judaism, even in these times of political differences.

Zionism in the postmodern era will cease to be a political movement; it already has the potential of a spiritual force. Its old Adam-the-first slogan "Never again!" sounds increasingly hollow, and the connection between the Holocaust and sovereignty, increasingly superficial. Only to the extent that Zionist theory will be able to integrate Adam the second, will Israel find a formula for co-existence that neither the premodernists — the so-called ultra-Orthodox halachists — nor the modernists — the secularists and the radical "left" of Reform Judaism — have been able to affirm.

The contention that Jewish law is no longer central to normative Jewish life does not mean that observance has ceased to matter to Jews. On the contrary. There is a growing tendency among non-halachic Jews to seek meaningful ways of living in Jewish time by observing Shabbat and festivals, and by marking significant events in their lives. There is also a growing commitment to the *mitzvah* of *talmud torah*, serious Jewish study. Today, many young Jewish families are much more observant and much more knowledgeable than their parents were, even when the parents paid more lip service to *halachah*.

Nor does it mean that the need to speak to God has ceased. Even those who have rejected the chaotic synagogue services of their childhood, or the sterile alternatives that they may have once preferred — because they were more comprehensible, though not more inspiring — continue to search for forms of worship that speak the language of Jewish tradition and meet the needs of postmodern Jewish men and women. In this respect, like in so many other areas of Jewish life today, the old denominational divisions make little sense.

These men and women realize that since they are only Adam the first, they are incomplete. They have to recognize in themselves Adam the second — the vulnerable, lonely dimension of human existence — and reach out to each other and to God in search of wholeness through holiness. As the reservations about the prowess of Adam the first of civil religion grow, so does the affirmation of Adam the second of piety increase.

Thus, for example, while many Orthodox Jews in North America are grappling with the need to abolish discrimination against women in their synagogues, Reform Jews are putting on *kippot* and *tallitot* and creating *chavurot*. These groups of like-minded Jews, who come together to *daven* Orthodox-style without the benefit of clergy, are in search of what they term "spirituality" and "religious living." It is in these groups, not in rallies on behalf of Israel or in Holocaust memorial meetings, that Jewish life is being renewed. It is the common quest, rather than the denominational line of demarcation, that brings these people closer to God. It is the desire to move from the halachic to the liturgical framework that makes for greater commitment to Judaism.

In trying to understand this phenomenon, I have been greatly helped by the writings of Lawrence Hoffman. One of his books is a popular practical guide for anyone seeking to meet the needs of Adam the second through prayer. It is aptly called *The Art of Public Prayer: Not For Clergy Only*.[19] The book cuts across the accepted boundaries of Jewish denominational divisions, of laypeople and professionals, and Jews and gentiles. It tries to address the needs of postmodern people and show how some of these needs can be met through symbolism, observance, liturgy and community.

It is not a coincidence that Hoffman is a professor of liturgy at the Hebrew Union College-Jewish Institute of Religion in New York, the institution that trains Reform rabbis, cantors and educators. Only a movement not committed to the traditional discipline of *halachah* can address the kind of issues with which Hoffman deals. Yet, I would be less than truthful were I to report a dramatic turning away from civility towards piety in our Reform circles. Yes, there are signs that Adam the second may be given a vote in our deliberations but, so far, Adam the first retains his veto and continues to dominate.

Even when we articulate the dangers of that domination, we seem to lack the courage to displace it. Our religious life continues to base itself on institutions, not on intuition.

Sadly, those who do challenge Adam the first with resolve tend to reject him, and move from modernity towards a premodern Judaism. This premodern Judaism, in its most Americanized form — despite its unAmerican name: Lubavitch — threatens to "proclaim" the Messiah, thus taking us back to the seventeenth century when another false Messiah, Sabbatai Zevi, was proclaimed. It was a very disturbed and unhappy epoch in Jewish history.

Nevertheless, despite the slow progress and the embarrassing setbacks, the trends are unmistakable. And here we no longer have to confine ourselves to the evidence from Jewish sources only. The authors of *Megatrends 2000* — far removed from the philosophy of Taylor, the politics of Havel, the sociology of Bauman, or the theology of Borowitz — point in a similar direction.[20] They identify trends in the 1990s that are moving away from what I have ventured to call civility towards what I have described as piety. They speak, for example, of a move from the quest for knowledge to the search for values, from the pre-occupation with physical recreation towards spiritual creativity, and from management to true leadership; in other words, from Adam the first to Adam the second.

Such trends are bound to greatly affect every manifestation of Judaism that wishes to describe itself as contemporary. By placing values before knowledge, we will be changing the direction of Jewish education from information *about* Judaism to commitment *to* Judaism. By paying less attention to the body of Adam the first and more to the soul of Adam the second, we will be shaping a different kind of Jewish community; a community less concerned with the fitness classes in the Jewish country club and more with the study groups in the synagogue; a community, not only prepared to guard the synagogue from the outside when on security duty, but ready to go inside to pray for God's protection.

But even more profound will be the impact of what *Megatrends 2000* calls the shift from management to leadership. In a penetrating study of the dynamics of synagogue and church, Rabbi Edwin Friedman suggests that true leadership should not be based on what one can make others do, but on what one *is* oneself.[21] The age of civility needs managers of Adam the first type; the age of piety will depend on leaders in Adam the second category. To the extent that we can already identify such leaders in our own midst, we can also measure the progress of our agenda. For all my misgivings about what I see around me — and, alas, within myself — I am not without hope.

Plaut's division of the history of Reform Judaism into four phases concluded with what he called "a tentative forecast for a fifth." Having surveyed the past, he dared look into the future by suggesting that "while the resuscitation of an 18th century pietism is surely inappropriate, some turning inward is necessary, and commitment or *mitzvah* are its twin anchors of expression." He concluded by asking: "What will phase five have in store for us?" and he continued, "I know what I would like it to be. I would like it to respond to the urgent question of *Ma yomru ba-meromim?* 'What do they say on high?' " The effort to describe the movement from civility to piety is an attempt to respond to this question.

In the light of this response, let us look again at Plaut's first four phases of Reform Judaism and suggest they can be reformulated with an eye on the future. First, when we will seek to answer "What will tradition say?" we need no longer defend ourselves with halachic arguments to affirm our status as the custodians of Israel's covenant with God. Second, when articulating Judaism for non-Jews, we will not need to engage in apologetics but, instead, seek genuine co-operation based on mutuality and symmetry. Third, when providing Jewish education to ensure Jewish continuity, we will address ourselves to both Adams, thus combining knowledge *about,* with experience *of,* what it is to be a Jew. And finally, when exploring the meaning of our own lives, we will try to add to the therapeutic-narcissistic the collective expression of *mitzvah.*

Notes

1 W. Gunther Plaut, "Reform Judaism: Past, Present and Future," *Journal of Reform Judaism* 28:3 (Summer, 1980).

2 *Beyond Survival* (London: Darton Longman & Todd, 1982), 203f; *Walking Toward Elijah* (Burlington, Ontario: Welch Publishing Company, 1988), 118f; *The Star of Return* (New York: Greenwood Press, 1991), xif.

3 Plaut, 1ff.

4 Jonathan S. Woocher, *Sacred Survival: The Civil Religion of American Jews* (Bloomington and Indianapolis: Indiana University Press, 1986).

5 Ibid., 63ff.

6 See Robert N. Bellah et al., *Habits of the Heart: Individualism and Commitment in American Life* (New York: Harper & Row, 1985), 71ff.

7 Christopher Lasch, *The Culture of Narcissim* (London: Abacus, 1980).

8 Woocher, 92.

9 Ibid., 93.

10 Ibid., 159.

11 Ibid., 160.

12 Ibid., 163.

13 Charles Taylor, *The Malaise of Modernity* (Concord, Ontario: Anansi Press, 1991).

14 Zygmunt Bauman, *Modernity and the Holocaust* (Ithaca, NY: Cornell University Press, 1989).

15 Eugene B. Borowitz, *Renewing the Covenant: A Theology for the Postmodern Jew* (Philadelphia: The Jewish Publication Society, 1991), 20.

16 See Joseph B. Soloveitchik, *The Lonely Man of Faith* (New York: Doubleday, 1992).

17 See Joseph B. Soloveitchik, *Halakhic Man* (Philadelphia: The Jewish Publication Society of America, 1983).

18 Borowitz, 282.

19 Lawrence A. Hoffman, *The Art of Public Prayer: Not for Clergy Only* (Washington, D.C.: The Pastoral Press, 1988).

20 John Naisbitt and Patricia Aburdene, *Megatrends 2000* (New York: Avon Books, 1990).

21 Edwin H. Friedman, *Generation to Generation: Family Process in Church and Synagogue* (New York: The Guilford Press, 1985), 2ff.

4

Assertive Judaism

Rabbi W. Gunther Plaut's five phases of Reform Judaism point to five fundamental issues that still challenge us.[1] Each arose in response to given historic situations, but now they are all part of our Reform agenda. Reform Judaism is today preoccupied with questions about tradition, the non-Jewish world, continuity, personal fulfilment and spirituality.

What follows is an attempt to respond to each of them, not defensively and apologetically, but assertively.

Tradition

How do we assert Reform Judaism in the face of the demands of tradition? In the same way as the founders of our movement set out to do it. Through careful study of the sources, they showed that Reform belongs to the mainstream of Judaism. We must not justify our existence by pointing to the shortcomings of other religious movements in Judaism, especially Orthodoxy. Instead, we must repeatedly stress the authenticity of our own position. We are at least as much the heirs of the prophets and sages as any other movement in Judaism. That we differ from others does not mean we must defend ourselves, or attack, because our understanding of Judaism implies and affirms pluralism. There are many ways to the God of Abraham, Isaac and Jacob; ours is one of them.

Address to the Biennial of the Pacific Northwest Council of the Union of American Hebrew Congregations, Portland, Oregon, March 31, 1989.

Reform education must provide the evidence. However, the fact that our educational endeavours concentrate so much on children makes that virtually impossible. Of course, the children are our future, the guarantors of continuity, but Judaism is too sophisticated and too complex to make sense to kids. It is a mature pursuit for mature adults. Children can be taught skills, but only adults can be given the intellectual tools that make for convictions.

One reason why we so often express our Judaism defensively is because we are uncertain of our ground, insecure, ignorant. Our Judaism is infantile because we learned it usually before we were 13. That is why our responses in later years remain immature. Imagine if all you and I knew about sex is what we learned before we were 13, or even 16! Judaism is at least as complex. Therefore, without a continuous programme of education, assertive Judaism will remain beyond us.

And so will our claim to authenticity. One of the characteristic features of Jewish tradition is its commitment to a lifetime of learning. A Jew who does not study, stunts his or her religious growth. Effort is valued more than achievement in our tradition as Judaism offers no degrees, no qualifications — only encouragement to delve deeper into the sources and thus grow taller as Jews.

I have a shrewd suspicion that had we, as a movement, been more committed — not merely on paper but in practice — to continued adult study, we would have curbed some excesses that threaten to drive us into the margin of Jewish life. To the extent that Reform Judaism today is becoming more "traditional," it is because more Reform Jews take adult study seriously. Jewish minimalism and Jewish ignorance are twins.

The Non-Jewish World

According to Plaut, the second phase of Reform, after tradition, was the preoccupation with being acceptable to the gentile world. Many Reform ideas and practices, which have by now become characteristics of our movement, have their origins in this preoccupation.

At times, it is dangerously defensive. Too often, we are too anxious to make a good impression on our gentile neighbours, believing that their criteria and standards are the correct ones. Defensiveness easily turns us into assimilationists.

The sad thing is that most gentiles despise Jews who want to obliterate their Jewishness or imitate non-Jews. As a result, many Jews who so desperately try to be accepted by non-Jews experience much anti-Semitism. That confuses them and, at times, they act irrationally. For example, they turn against the ultra-Orthodox who allegedly through their distinctive garb, characteristic language and demonstrative behaviour are giving Jews a bad name. Another manifestation of the confusion is to see anti-Semitism everywhere and to get indignant in the wrong places and at inappropriate times. Sometimes, even our allegiance to Israel stems from the same neurosis. Some Jews want Israel to be perfect, yet not very Jewish. They secretly want to shape it in an idealized WASP image.

Assertive Judaism is different. It teaches us to have enough self-confidence in what we are, warts and all. Our attitude to Israel is a case in point. Defensiveness makes us support every Israeli government policy, however wrong. It also makes us threaten withdrawal of all support if Israeli policies offend us. We vacillate aimlessly between these extremes. Assertiveness, on the other hand, liberates us to be critical of whatever merits our strictures. It does this without threats to our Israeli brothers and sisters and without apologies to our non-Jewish neighbours.

The existence of Israel is, I believe, the focal point of our existence as Jews: God is the centre of humanity, Torah the centre of Judaism; the State of Israel the centre of the Jewish people. We need not apologize to the opponents of God, Torah or the Jewish state, but we must struggle with each of these givens of Judaism assertively and honestly. We must allow our own criteria to inform our judgement, and not judge Jewish behaviour by standards imposed from the outside.

As assertive Jews, we can take our place as partners in the society in which we live and fight for justice and goodness for all. We can fight not for reasons of public relations so that people in high places should think well of us Jews, but on intrinsic merits no matter whether it gains us popularity. Emancipation does not mean assimilation — aping the values of others — but integration, articulating the values and ideals of our own tradition, and doing so with the passion of the biblical prophets and the consistency of rabbinic sages.

Continuity

This is the outlook I would like us to teach our children. I referred earlier to the futility of infantilizing Judaism. Now I wish to speak of the nobility of presenting it to future generations as a way of life for us, the adults, as something that we are not just "proud of" when anti-Semites attack us — letting them decide our identity — but something we feel passionately about when times are good and alternatives are freely available. Our aim must be to imbue the young with a commitment to Judaism that is not based on a ghetto-siege mentality, but one that presupposes the free and open society for which we all strive and in which we all thrive.

Such freedom must also mean that we do not necessarily exercise all options available to us. If I am truly free, I must be able to set boundaries for myself. And if the society in which I live is truly tolerant, it must not impose conformity and uniformity on me. The assertive Jew will have subjected himself or herself to a discipline by which the values of our religion can be made manifest and the sancta of our tradition made visible. If freedom forces people to obliterate their peculiarities in order to be integrated, it soon becomes a new kind of totalitarianism. Therefore, it is only as observant Jews that we can be assertive Jews; observant Reform Jews, of course.

It is in this way, too, that we can act as role models for our children. Only if they see, with their own eyes, that Judaism matters to their parents, will it matter to them. Only if they witness the significance of Jewish values and Jewish practices for their parents, will they recognize the opportunities these values and practices offer their own lives.

If the only Judaism they see is what the teacher teaches in religious school, it will be virtually pointless. Think back on what you actually remember of what you were taught in public school at the age of 10! Had we not used reading and writing since those days, it is unlikely we would be literate today. And had we not seen our parents read and write, it is unlikely we would have wanted to do the same. Our general education is largely bound up with parental behaviour and attitudes. Why should Jewish education be different?

Unless our children are encouraged by example to use the skills acquired in religious school, the entire enterprise will have been futile. No wonder that, according to many surveys, Hebrew school students often know less Hebrew in the higher grades than they knew in the lower ones. A sense of futility is a powerful disincentive. If you only experience a Jewish festival in religious school, and not as a part of the life of your family, you will soon identify it as a boring game and opt out. If Jewish observance is perceived as a kids' game, the aim will be to grow up and be like daddy and mommy as soon as possible, that is, non-observant.

Assertive Judaism is also the opposite of vicarious Judaism: it is my Judaism, not the Judaism of my ancestors, or of my Israeli cousins, or even of my children.

Personal Fulfilment

Addressing the question, "What will tradition say?" I spoke of authenticity. Addressing the question, "What will the gentiles say?" I spoke of dignity. In answer to the third question, "What will the children say?" I spoke of responsibility. Turning to the more personal question, "What will my life say?" let me speak of integrity, to be more precise, the integrity of my Jewish personality.

Teachers as diverse as Abraham Joshua Heschel, the Jewish thinker, and Erich Fromm, the psychotherapist, have written that our modern lives are poor in being and abundant in having.[2] Ours is a consumer world, and we apply consumerism to religion too. The result has been, according to Canadian sociologist Reginald Bibby, that the western world has developed a system of religion à la carte.[3] In our context, this means that we do not relate to tradition in search of authenticity, but choose bits and pieces that take our fancy. Current practices among Reform Jews, for example, reveal an unbelievable hodge-podge. Our attitude to the gentile world is equally strange. We imitate when we should desist, and desist when co-operation is called for. When it comes to teaching our children, our idiosyncrasies border on the bizarre. And when it comes to our own lives, the vestiges and fragments of Judaism that are included often lack coherence.

The Hebrew word *kedusha*, translated as 'holiness,' implies separation, having the integrity to stand apart. The English word "holiness" has often been juxtaposed with "wholeness," which is yet another word for integrity. Religion in general, and Judaism in particular, will bring us little joy if we approach it in the same way as we tackle the grocery shelf in the supermarket: letting taste and economics decide our faith. If traditional authenticity, dignity in the face of the non-Jewish world and responsibility to the next generation count for little, integrity will be lacking.

That is how we must understand recent efforts to place religious commitment and religious living in the centre of Reform Judaism. They reflect the determination of our leadership to counteract the tepid civil religion into which many of us have fled. They shy away from reducing us to nameless and faceless donors to Jewish causes, who pay lip service to tradition, to the gentile world and to the children's Jewish commitment as manifestations of civil religion. The leadership of our movement has called us to step forward as individuals and seek to make Judaism relevant to our own lives. We are called upon not only to vote in committees, but to testify at services; not only to choose, but to discipline ourselves, to subject ourselves voluntarily to the obligations that *mitzvot* make on us. Reform Judaism needs no legal code, only responsible adherents who impose duties on themselves.

Spirituality

That is the stuff of which spirituality is made. This fifth rubric is the product of our endeavours as authentic, dignified and responsible Jews who show integrity in our own lives. An assertive Jew stands before God in prayer. The Hebrew *lehitpallel*, 'to pray,' does not have the petitionary connotation of the English, for it means "to plead one's case." Assertive Judaism enables us, entitles us, to plead our case to elicit an affirmative answer from on high.

Notes

1 W. Gunther Plaut, "Reform Judaism: Past, Present and Future," *Journal of Reform Judaism*, 28:3 (Summer 1980).

2 Erich Fromm, *To Have Or To Be* (New York: Harper & Row, 1976) and Abraham Joshua Heschel, *The Sabbath* (Philadelphia: Jewish Publication Society of America, 1963).

3 Reginald W. Bibby, *Fragmented Gods* (Toronto: Irwin Publishing, 1987), especially chapter 4.

5

Judaism in America: Critical Impressions

Jewish labels are misleading. What was considered Liberal Judaism in Germany is often described as Reform in Britain and Conservative in North America. The equivalent to British Liberal Judaism is supposed to be Reform on the other side of the Atlantic. And then we have "Progressive," used for combinations of the above.

Based on this description, members of Reform congregations in England should join Conservative congregations when they go to live in the United States. But those who do, are often disappointed and very soon switch to Reform temples. The reasons for the confusion are several.

Although most British Jews find the American Reform ambience very strange, especially at prayer — due to the prayerbook, with its peculiar English, the music and the bare-headed men — they are less maladjusted there than in the Conservative synagogue. The situation on the west coast of the United States, where everything is more "left," may be different, yet the generalization holds. If you are a member of a Reform congregation in Britain, you will likely end up in a Reform one in America. Although, on paper, you may think you are closer to Conservative Judaism, you will be more at home in American Reform, despite its similarities to Liberal Judaism in Britain.

Originally entitled "How Women Hoisted Reform into the Lead" when it appeared in *Manna* (Autumn, 1987).

This brings us to the malaise in Conservative Judaism: its theology is often at odds with its practice. Although its basic tenets are non-fundamentalist and close to Reform, its constituent bodies tend to model themselves on modern Orthodox counterparts seeking to fill the place that is being vacated by neo-Orthodoxy. Conservative Judaism may think *trefah*, yet it eats not only *kosher* but, nowadays, even *glatt kosher*.

As Orthodoxy has gone more to the "right," it has squeezed out the moderates in its ranks. Rabbi Irving Greenberg, the celebrated Orthodox moderate, may receive an enthusiastic reception at the annual conference of Reform Synagogues of Great Britain, but he is often shunned in Orthodox circles. There seems to be no room for his open and tolerant approach in a world increasingly dominated by extremism.

Conservative Judaism has sought to fill the middle ground Orthodoxy seeks to destroy. As a result, its synagogues have become more Orthodox: traditional prayerbooks are replacing those published by the Conservative movement; English has virtually disappeared from its services; two days of festivals are usually observed; and *kippot* are always worn by men in the *shul* building, not only at services. As I was writing this, a Conservative colleague called to say that he and his wife will be pleased to come to dinner, but could the meal be without meat. Although they do not question the *kashrut* in our home, they observe the Orthodox tradition of not eating meat during the nine days before *Tisha b'Av*. It is not something one would, until now, have expected from a Conservative rabbi.

Services in American Conservative Synagogues are often close to the *minhag* of the United Synagogue in London as it was before it went "right." Significantly, the "cathedral" of Conservative Judaism in Britain, the New London Synagogue, is at pains to remind us that it is the custodian of that British *minhag*, 'tradition,' and not an American importation. For very good reasons, it does not even like the term Conservative. Like its satellite congregations, it is a much greater threat to Anglo-Jewish Orthodoxy, to whose adherents it offers a more moderate alternative, than to Reform, to whose members it looks very much like the Orthodoxy they reacted against in the first place. From my Canadian perspective, the few Reform

Jews who seem attracted to this middle-of-the-road Judaism reflect nostalgia rather than theology.

When such people cross the Atlantic, they may, at first, be fooled by the "progressive" nature of Conservative Judaism. Only a part of the weekly *sidra* is read on Shabbat, the car park is open and men and women sit together. But they soon discover that it is far from Reform in Britain and that the rabbi has very strong Orthodox leanings, especially if he is a product of the Jewish Theological Seminary, which, for a long time, has been on the right of the movement.

Lately, however, there has been a remarkable shift, at least in one important area. The Seminary has agreed to ordain female rabbis and invest female cantors. By that, it has greatly modified its orientation and placed itself, inadvertently perhaps, in the Reform camp, despite all halachic arguments in favour of female rabbis. It is unrealistic to court Orthodoxy in the present religious–political climate in Israel and the Diaspora and, simultaneously, put females on a *Beit Din,* a Jewish court of law.

This step came as a severe blow to many Conservative Jews who were anxious to keep their distance from Reform in hope of being accepted by Orthodoxy. This hope is particularly strong in Israel. There, although the Orthodox establishment attacks both movements as if they were one, Conservative Jews expect to gain some recognition if they do not associate with Reform more than is necessary for the semblance of preserving *kelal Yisrael,* Jewish unity. Hence the spectacle of the Orthodox establishment in Israel treating Conservative Judaism as if it were Reform, while Conservative Jews try to appear as Orthodox as possible, sometimes even surreptitiously pointing an accusing finger at Reform.

Ordination of women by the Seminary has not only given Orthodox opponents all the ammunition they need, but it has precipitated a potential breakaway of the right wing of the Conservative movement. This may lead to further polarization: one side joining Reform, the other replacing modern Orthodoxy. What sociologists have predicted for some time — the possible breakup of Conservative Judaism despite its numerical strength — may now come about. Recognizing that a religious movement cannot exist without a consistent theological stance, and that the middle ground in religion is invariably shaky, experts have predicted polarization. We have no reason to rejoice, for the prediction only reflects the tendency to replace clear *thinking* with confused *doing*, and so move to the right.

In religion, you can be crazy, even lazy, but not hazy. It seems that Conservative Judaism is paying a price for its haziness so that even the alleged laziness of Reform seems more attractive.

The reason why the ordination of women has contributed to the potential split in Conservative Judaism must be sought in the remarkable growth of American Reform. Despite theological weakness and a tendency to anarchy, Reform has made enormous strides in the recruitment of members and rabbis, in building institutions and in initiating projects.

Much of this is due to the emergence of women as lay and rabbinic leaders of the movement. Conservative Judaism saw that it was losing many of its best people to Reform because egalitarianism and feminism are central issues in contemporary America. In the choice between possible atrophy and probable polarization, it chose the latter. It is too early to tell if it was worth it. Most of those who join Reform congregations today are young families who grew up Conservative but no longer feel at home there. It is doubtful whether the presence of Conservative women rabbis will be sufficient to reverse the trend.

The influx of members with more traditional backgrounds is affecting Reform. Much of the swing to the right — acceptance of *kippot* and *tallitot* as legitimate options at prayer, *kashrut* at Synagogue functions, greater stress on Hebrew and the study of texts; and observance of second day *Rosh Hashana* in some places — has been initiated by these new member families. Of course, this has often given rise to tension within congregations between "the young upstarts" and "the old guard," but not on the same scale as the rift in the Conservative movement. Reform has been strengthened by the tension and it speaks today with greater confidence than ever.

The reason why some Reform Jews should nevertheless be tempted to flirt with Conservative Judaism is not difficult to discern. They fear anarchy in the Reform movement and the danger of minimal observance among its members. It is a legitimate fear that none of us can ignore. However, the remedy may be worse than the disease. It seeks to cure one extreme — everybody making *Shabbos* for themselves — with another — Orthodoxy determining how *Shabbos* should be made. It may be easier to fight Reform anarchy from within than to seek to replace it with rigidity. Self-scrutiny and self-criticism are helpful in trying to make Reform not only relevant but authentic. Imitation of other movements will polarize us just as Conservative Judaism became polarized when it tried to imitate Orthodoxy.

As American Reform has grown in strength, it has become more open to self-scrutiny. There is an acute awareness of the danger of anarchy and a growing insistence on religious content, not only popular form. It is this that has made Reform so exciting for me. I will suffer the liturgy for the sake of the search and I can endure the empty pews because of the full classrooms.

The more I observe American Reform and work within it, the more conscious I become that it runs the risk of becoming a sect, which, in time may be relegated to oblivion. But I can also see that it contains the possibility of becoming the normative Judaism of tomorrow. To participate in the endeavour on behalf of the latter option is exhilarating.

6

In God's Name: Law as a Religious Category

In *Real Presences*, George Steiner, the distinguished literary critic, asserts that the basis of all aesthetic appreciation is the assumption that God exists.[1] Without this affirmation, nothing significant can have meaning in the lives of individuals or in society. Human creativity only makes sense, according to Steiner, when it is based on the recognition that we are created in the image of God.

Though neither a theologian nor an exponent of organized religion, as a student of the creative process, Steiner is compelled to take God seriously. He does so, not out of *a priori* premises, but because of inescapable conclusions. He writes that "where God's presence is no longer a tenable supposition and where His absence is no longer a felt — indeed, overwhelming weight — certain dimensions of thought and creativity are no longer attainable." The spoken and written word is the primary vehicle for the attainment of these dimensions. For, as Steiner puts it, "it is in sacred texts, in laws, in literature that civilization is housed."[2]

Steiner's inductive method, which leads him from the appreciation of artistic creativity to the contemplation of divine essence, is

Reprinted from the *Gazette* of the Law Society of Upper Canada, 25:1 (March 1991), based on an address at the Interfaith Service to mark the opening of the courts in Ontario, January 7, 1991, at the Metropolitan United Church, Toronto.

highly conducive to the enterprise that has brought us together today. He suggests that it is possible, indeed inevitable, for human beings who have passed through the ordeal of modernity to affirm God. It is possible, not because we have been programmed to do so by this or that institution or denomination, as was the case in the premodern era, but because we have honestly and carefully sought to understand the texts on which our culture is founded.

The sensitive poet thus becomes a prophet and the sensible lawyer, a priest. I stand here to remind you of your priestly calling. For better or worse, you and I are in the same business. Our encounter in this place of worship today is much more than a mere nod to an archaic custom.

I speak out of a tradition that has always regarded the administration of law as a task rooted in the covenant between humanity and God. In this scheme of things, the practice of law is considered a religious activity. The seemingly plural Hebrew word *Elohim,* means 'God' and 'judges.' Whenever it is used in Scripture, rabbinic tradition understands it to refer to the divine attribute of justice. We may, therefore, infer that whenever justice is applied God is present. The practice of law is a religious activity.

The identification of the legal with the divine is, incidentally, one reason why the enemies of Judaism have sought to denigrate the Torah, the body of Jewish teaching, by describing it as "mere law," and Judaism as a religion of law. What these detractors have failed to recognize is that it is not God's word that is being reduced to law. It is law that has been elevated to the realm of the sacred.

With this as background, let us now look at a sentence in the Torah that begins: *"Tzedek, tzedek tirdof...,"* 'Justice, justice shall you pursue, that you may thrive and occupy the land that the Lord your God is giving you' (Deuteronomy 16:20). On the assumption that no word is frivolous or superfluous in Scripture, Jewish sages have asked why the word, *tzedek,* 'justice,' is repeated. By recognizing that the same word, *tzedek,* can have two grammatical forms, they concluded that the verse should be read to mean: Justice by means of justice shall you pursue. The divine quality of justice is only operative if the humanly created instruments of justice — the laws — are just. In this way, any possible division between the pursuit of justice and the practice of law has been eliminated. The distinction between morality and legality is obliterated. The cleric and the lawyer are not in conflict with each other but are, in fact, the same person. The law as a creation of the human legislative process is only authentic if it is a response to the divine command.

This may sound like a reiteration of the ancient doctrine that sought to make every discipline the handmaiden of theology. However, I am trying to say the opposite. I am admitting the inadequacy of conventional religious institutions by implying that, since the advent of modernity, they have largely ceased to dominate human affairs. Even ritual has been secularized: more people testify to a sense of the sacred and the transcendent in the stadium or the shopping mall than in church or synagogue. A court house inspires a greater sense of awe than a house of worship.

We live in a postmodern world. Modernity caused secularization and distance from conventional religion. The postmodern era has made us realize that God is not dead, although many religious institutions are gasping for breath, but that God is present in everything we do that has meaning. And that most certainly includes the practice of law.

The traditional diploma of a rabbi concludes with the words, "He may teach, he may teach; he may judge, he may judge." It reflects the premodern age, when law belonged to the realm of religion. The rabbinic seminary in Britain that ordained me has eliminated the words, "He may judge, he may judge." I make no claim to legal expertise. As a product of the modern era, my only qualification is that of a teacher of Jewish tradition; I accept that the judging is done by others.

My lack of real authority has given me a measure of freedom, but it has also relegated me, as an exponent of organized religion, to the margin of society. I can still study texts and explain them, but I have no power to decide the just course of action. However, instead of waging quixotic battles between religious teachings and legal enactments, I wish to make common cause; to restore the teaching and the judging, if not in the same person, then in a mutually beneficial partnership.

I believe that the postmodern era, with its renewed affirmation of God, may bring us closer to that partnership; that the traditions from which the priest, the imam and the rabbi speak, have something to say to those who shape our society — no longer in impotent prophetic admonition, but in measured priestly guidance and co-operation. We cannot return to the premodern past, and we must not be imprisoned by the modern present. We must go beyond both into the postmodern future in which co-operation replaces competition and strife.

In that future, we are compelled to view our common task not only by what is acceptable and expedient, but by what is eternally valid, however interpreted and administered at any given moment. Law can neither be subsumed by religion nor divorced from it; its task is to reflect divine truth in human application.

Natural law, in the tradition out of which I speak, is invariably supranatural, even supernatural. "This, indeed, is the distinctive contribution of Israel's thinkers to the discussion of natural law," writes William A. Irwin. "For them, it was not an irresponsible force that in some blind way, however benignly, influenced human impulses." And he continues: "It was God, in his holiness and righteousness, revealing to sinful man his will and their high destiny and only happiness in obedience thereto. From this, there resulted all that is characteristic of Hebrew ethics."[3] Just as the literary critic realizes that human discourse is not a matter of word games, but of transcendent meaning, the lawyer acknowledges that the administration of human affairs is not a matter of convention and politics, but of the will of God as revealed in the texts that regulate these affairs. If these texts appear archaic it is because, in the words of Steiner, "they carry in them the pulse of the distant source."[4]

The will of the people through the democratic process remains paramount, of course. Yet with Steiner, we must reject "the American genius that would democratize eternity" and affirm that God speaks to us when we pursue justice with justice.[5] In this way, we place law, not only outside politics, but in the realm that is above politics, in the same realm as religion. Religion and law must, of course, be subject to the political process, but they become corrupt when they are invaded by political power.

Neither the modern world nor its predecessor has known how to withstand such invasions, and many of the tragedies in history are the result. Will the postmodern world fare better? The prospect of a division of responsibility between teaching God's word and administering God's laws in a democratic state, coupled with the realization that the practitioners of each need each other, may make it legitimate to answer this question with a resounding "Yes." We may, indeed, be entering a new era in which the artificial barrier between the divine and the human, the religious and the secular, will be replaced by a more diffuse, but accurate, differentiation between the holy and the not-yet sanctified.

Notes

1 George Steiner, *Real Presences* (London: Faber and Faber, 1989).

2 Ibid.

3 William A. Irwin, *The Old Testament: Keystone of Human Culture* (London: Abelard-Schuman, 1959), 149.

4 Steiner, 28.

5 Ibid., 33.

7

Halachah and Reform Judaism

The difference between the sacred and the profane in our tradition is a matter of lines of demarcation. That is already implied in the meaning of the biblical word *kadosh*, 'to set apart.' We *sanctify* by setting something apart from the rest, and, when we step over the limit, we move from the realm of the sacred into the profane, or vice versa.

The *halachah* came to codify the rules pertaining to the lines of demarcation in its emphasis on *issur* and *heter*, that which is forbidden and that which is allowed. The clarification of the borders between the prohibited and the permitted has remained the principal aim of the halachic process today.

The trouble with borders, however, is that they create fences. Hence the *siyag*, 'fence,' around the Torah. And fences often imprison in the guise of protecting. Reform Judaism correctly perceived much of *halachah* as a prison that inhibited Jews and Judaism. The Reform approach to *halachah* was to free its captives and, thus, release Jewish creativity.

It has achieved much of what it set out to do. The question is now whether it can retain its gains, or if they will be squandered; whether the victory over what was perceived as halachic tyranny may not deteriorate into liberal/libertine anarchy; whether the protest against unjust fences will become the tearing down of barriers altogether,

Based on a paper submitted to the Responsa Committee of the Central Conference of American Rabbis in 1992.

thus making Judaism indistinguishable from other religions. Our opponents accuse us of precisely that, and they may have to be put in their place by way of apologetics. But that does not mean that their strictures should always be ignored, for they may not be totally unwarranted.

This essay tries to describe some lines of demarcation between the holy and the profane, the permitted and the prohibited, as guidelines for our Reform halachic decisions. Although we may be living in a "post-halachic" age — that is, at a time when Jewish law has ceased to be legally binding for Jews — we must still take *halachah* seriously, even when we choose not to follow it. For Jewish law, even when no longer operative, still forms the very foundation of our tradition.

To describe lines of demarcation is no easy task. Once Reform Jews question not only what is the authentic word of God, but if God speaks to us at all through *halachah* — what are the criteria for defining (that is, limiting) the borders? What follows is an attempt to promote discussion by identifying four markers.

First, on the assumption that *mitzvah,* commandment, is fundamental to our understanding of Judaism, we have reason to regard traditional practice, *minhag avotenu veimmotenu beyadenu*, the practices of our ancestors, as a marker. Even if tradition only has a vote, not a veto, it seems reasonable not to go against it, unless there are compelling reasons for doing so. Although it is not always clear what is tradition and what is not, we must try to uphold the principle that whatever our historic research identifies as tradition should be considered a marker in our endeavour to describe decisions and actions as authentically Jewish.

Take *Shabbat* observance, for example. As much as we may legitimately decide that the halachic fences around Sabbath observance no longer enhance the celebration of the day, and as much as we may want to make the distinction between the divine commandment to keep the Sabbath and the human laws in response to that commandment, as they have evolved over time, there must be some defined limits beyond which Saturday ceases to be *Shabbat*. Even if we do not believe that it is "the Lord's day" literally, tradition has nevertheless set limits about how *Shabbat* should be observed.

True, it may not be possible or desirable to impose observance on our members. But, surely, it is incumbent upon us not only to describe its nature, but also define (and thus limit) it in the manner of *halachah*. In so doing, we would set norms and standards, not to impose them on our constituents over whom we have no power at all, but to articulate our understanding of Judaism, and thus offer guidance to those who wish to take it.

A second criterion for setting limits would be *knesset Yisrael*, the well-being and unity of the Jewish polity. *Shabbat* has limits and Jews are not to "make *Shabbos* for themselves."

Take the issue of Jewish status. Whatever its historic origins and subsequent changes, Jewish tradition has developed criteria for who is a member of *knesset Yisrael*. Changing these criteria may lead to a separation within the Jewish people. When we are fighting for Jewish survival — and when we seek to introduce different criteria (for example, patrilineal descent) ostensibly to safeguard Jewish continuity — we cannot ignore most non-Reform Jews, even if we disagree with their stance.

Patrilineal descent may be democratic, just and biblical, but it is not where normative Judaism is today. It may be proper for us to fight for a change from within, but is it justified to go it alone? Is there not a danger that the possible institutional successes that the decision on patrilineality has brought to the Reform movement, may have detrimental long-term consequences for Reform in *knesset Yisrael?*

May it not reduce American Reform to a sect, since normative Judaism, whether we like it or not, is increasingly shaped by the State of Israel? And Israel, for better or worse, has remained within the traditional halachic framework, at least in matters of Jewish status.

And what about the practitioners of Reform Judaism outside the United States who do not share its conviction about patrilineal descent? Do they count for nothing because, in comparison with the United States, they are numerically insignificant?

When we speak of *knesset Yisrael,* it is not the vox populi we have in mind. Judaism has never decided issues by way of plebiscites. When the rabbis decreed, *acharey rabbim lehattot,* 'we must follow the majority,' they had in mind those competent to decide, not decisions to be taken at the ballot box. And today, whatever the popular view and common practice among Jews may be, most Jews we would regard as competent to decide will not side with patrilineal descent; even American Reform is split on the issue.

Third, a main reason for acknowledging the equality between patrilineal and matrilineal descent is *tzedek,* justice and righteousness. Even if tradition is unanimous about a practice, and even if the cognitive minority sanctions it as normative Judaism, if we are convinced that it is unjust, as Reform Jews we are duty-bound to seek to change it. And not only has the purpose to be *tzedek,* but so have the means: *tzedek tzedek tirdof — tzedek **b**'tzedek tirdof,* 'justice with just means shall you pursue.' As vague as the term "justice" may be, it is nevertheless an indispensable criterion in our decision-making process.

The status of women is a case in point. The consistent and courageous stance of Reform Judaism has not only brought into the tradition and the community many women who otherwise would have been alienated from both, but it has forced the other movements in Judaism to grapple with the issue. And it was not satisfied merely to give women certain rights in roundabout and underhanded ways. The means by which justice was to be pursued had also to be just.

The outlook of individual rabbis and the respective rabbinic bodies will determine the nature of their partisanship. Thus it is reasonable to expect, and fully consistent with the "post-halachic" stance of Reform Judaism, that the Central Conference of American Rabbis would pay greater attention to *tzedek* and *darchey shalom*, 'communal unity,' than to *minhag avotenu veimmotenu beyadenu* and *knesset Yisael.* That would make it different from its sister organizations.

But, surely, this does not mean that tradition and community must always yield. One way Reform rabbis can epitomize prophetic Judaism is by going against the grain and acting as correctives and critics to the unacceptable aspects of contemporary social trends. Even when we take expediency into account, we need not do it at the expense of other markers.

Fourth, it may also be possible to satisfy the demands of all, or most, lines of demarcation simultaneously by making the halachic distinction between *reshut hayachid,* 'private practice,' and *reshut harabbim,* 'public policy.'

We can probably meet the needs of our members by not castigating them for lax *Shabbat* observance in their homes, and yet maintain a standard of observance in our congregations that is traditional and consistent with practices in the community. Similarly, we may welcome individual Jews and, where needed, deal with their Jewish status in a manner appropriate to their circumstances. We can do so without making public pronouncements about how we intend to change the criteria for Jewishness, or disregard traditional notions of the conduct of rabbis.

We are, naturally, tempted to label such distinctions as hypocritical. But not to distinguish between individual conduct and collective standards may point to a legalistic literalism worthy of extreme Orthodoxy and unknown in our Reform tradition. A responsive and responsible *posek* or *poseket,* (a person deciding on matters of Jewish law) should be able to reconcile seemingly contrary demands, and remain firmly within the limits without putting up offensive fences and without deserving the charge of hypocrisy.

Zion

Though much in the earlier chapters of this book is about the centrality of Israel in contemporary Jewish life, the three essays that follow deal explicitly with the subject.

Their aim is to stress the historic opportunity before us to fuse the two modernist Jewish movements of our time: Reform and Zionism. By recognizing their affinity — earlier controversies and present misunderstandings notwithstanding — we may be able to identify the solid foundation on which the future of Judaism can be built.

The theoretical basis for this view can be found in Thomas Kuhn's understanding of paradigm shifts. Though Kuhn is a philosopher of science, his model has theological relevance and is applicable to understanding of the course of Jewish history.

I believe we are presently in the midst of a paradigm shift with enormous implication for Jewish thought and Jewish life. Jewish continuity is contingent upon our ability to acknowledge the shift and act accordingly.

8

Israel and the Diaspora

The nature of the land of Israel and its possession by the people of Israel is a fundamental preoccupation of the Torah. Therefore, it is also central to our understanding of our relationship to the State of Israel. Although the attitude of the Jewish people to the land of Israel has not been uniform or consistent through the ages, even less-than-friendly interpreters of the past concede that the land has always been central to us. It remains so more than ever in our time.

The land of Israel is not only a matter of interest to its inhabitants, but to all Jews committed to the Torah. A Jewish state in the land cannot be only a state for all its citizens, though it must never be less than that. It is also the state of the entire Jewish people. It is this conviction that gives us not only the right to speak about Israel, whether we live there or not, but also charges us with the duty to do so.

Using, as a starting point, an insight by Martin Buber, I have repeatedly argued that Judaism is always a triangle consisting of faith, people and land. Belief in God, allegiance to fellow-Jews and the quest for a permanent address in the world — Israel, no matter where we live in the Diaspora — are the three dimensions of our collective Jewish heritage. Only through the State of Israel can they come together as a whole.

This is a complex heritage and difficult to put into practice. To simplify it, many contemporary Jews cling to one of the three

Reprinted from *Viewpoints* 20:5 (1992). It was written when Israel had a Likud government led by Prime Minister Yitzchak Shamir.

dimensions only, at the expense of the other two. Hence the insistence by some that Judaism is primarily, if not exclusively, faith; by others that it is people; and by still others that you can only be a Jew if you live in the land of Israel. Many factions in contemporary Jewry can be divided this way. Accepting that Judaism is faith, people and land, in equal measure, would compel them to revise their existing allegiances. Few are prepared to do that.

But things are changing now that the Jewish state is a reality. For example, it is not a coincidence that in Canada, as elsewhere in the Diaspora, the Zionist organizations linked to synagogue communities — Mizrachi on behalf of modern Orthodoxy, Mercaz as an offshoot of Conservative Judaism and Kadima as the Zionist organization of Reform Jews — are thriving, while the old, secular, so-called political parties are still desperately trying to hold on to power.

The three mainstream movements in Judaism have accepted the triangular, multidimensional shape of Judaism. The others have not. They still operate in the mistaken secularist belief that Jews can be like all the other nations of the world. They ignore the fact that, in this way, they are rendering Judaism irrelevant. Why should anybody want to be Jewish only to be like everybody else, given that most Jews can assimilate and be someone else in much greater comfort and at much smaller risk? Therefore, it is those who see commitment to Israel as part of Judaism as a whole who are in a better position to formulate the new Zionism, as it is emerging after the establishment of the State of Israel.

The new Zionism affirms, by implication, the legitimacy of the Diaspora's concern for what happens in Israel. It entails support of and commitment to the Jewish state. It must never be less than that. But it also means partnership, perhaps even participation, by the Diaspora.

My affirmation of the land arises out of my religious commitment. This means I take seriously God's claim, "The land is Mine; you are but strangers resident with Me" (Leviticus 25:23). I am aware, however, that not only this sentence, but the chapter as a whole, can be taken in more than one way. The text gives legitimacy to those who say that, because the land belongs to God and we are only the custodians, it behooves us to behave according to the highest ethical standards. "You shall observe My laws and faithfully keep My rules, that you may live upon the land in security" (Leviticus 25:18).

Unfortunately, these texts also provide a scriptural basis for those who say that, having now repossessed the land, we are forbidden to give any of it back, irrespective of political exigences, because that would go against the will of God. The Lubavitcher rebbe and his religious opponents can quote the same passages for diametrically opposed conclusions. All that we can hope for is that the one will not accuse the other of heresy and apostasy because of different interpretations.

Of course, it is not the reading of texts that leads to convictions, but convictions that make us find in texts what we are looking for. Let me, therefore, admit what you will have already guessed. I am in tune with those aspects of our tradition that warn us against the exploitation of the land, the abuse of any of its citizens and the unwarranted attacks on any of its neighbours. "Do not wrong one another, but fear your God; for I the Lord am your God" (Leviticus 25:17).

It is this conviction that prompts me to support those forces that regard peace as so precious that they are even prepared to trade territory for it. Paradoxically, because the land is so central, some of it may have to be given up for the security of the rest. It is a difficult decision for a host of reasons, many of them connected to the fact that the enemies of the Jewish people may take advantage of the dissent.

The dissenter is also in danger of being ostracized by his or her own community, because, fearing anti-Semitism, many in the Jewish community, particularly in Canada, see it as their primary role to support the government of Israel, right or wrong. While we do not hesitate to criticize Canadian politicians or bureaucrats or law-enforcers, we are, at best, silent when power is abused by their Israeli counterparts.

The reason normally given for such docility is that, since we don't live in Israel, we are not allowed to be critical of its leaders. I don't share this view. I believe the Diaspora is a partner in Israel precisely because Israel is central to all Jewish life. And the same community does not hesitate to express criticism of other countries where Jews live and where Jewish values may be at risk.

The failure to speak our minds has exacerbated our relationship with our non-Jewish neighbours. Increasingly, they question our moral sensitivities that allow us to be so high-minded about others and so uncritical of our own. The irony should not escape us. In an effort not to give enemies grounds for pointing to our internal dissent, we are giving enemies *and* friends grounds for suspecting our moral will. That we defend ourselves by invoking our past suffering, especially the Holocaust, does not make the arguments stronger, only more pathetic. Precisely because we have been victims, we should know what it means to turn others into victims. Therefore, we should go out of our way to treat them as we would want to be treated ourselves.

So much for some reasons that prompt me to be a dissenter. I prefer the term "radical" because I take the word seriously: someone who goes to the root of the meaning of things. Our Jewish legacy compels us to go to our prophetic roots. It also warns us against making compromises for the sake of expediency.

But a radical is also an insider. A critic of Israel who remains uninvolved and uncommitted is like the wicked son in the Haggadah. Only those who share the responsibility have the right to dissent. But uncritical supporters of Israel, many of whom know little of its history and even less of its language and culture, may be substituting their enthusiasm for Judaism.

So what's the answer? Of course, there is no single answer, but a suggestion: to open the debate more fully; not to fear critical views of Israel and of each other, and not to hanker after the approval of Israeli politicians in power, even if it means the Prime Minister of Israel will be more reluctant to pose for photographers with the President of the Canadian Jewish Congress than he is with the emissaries of its arch-rival.

Independence of mind and action makes for communal health and increases the stature of Canadian Jewry. The absence of it will alienate many of its members.

At best, those alienated will keep silent and vote with their wallets — refusing to make contributions. More likely, they will want to speak out. Not to give them a voice is to deprive Israel of the support of true lovers of Zion.

Canadian Jewry cannot, must not, be built on the ever-decreasing number of those whose principal aim is to maintain the status quo. It must rely on a much broader base that today consists largely of university-trained professionals who are not afraid, as their parents were, of anti-Semitism and who are not prepared to mouth other people's views only because they have been formulated by Israelis.

9

New Directions for Zionism

Speaking in London, England, at the 1983 convention of the Zionist Federation of Great Britain and Ireland, Professor Anita Shapira of Tel Aviv University said that Zionism was born of the Jews' simultaneous encounter with modernity and anti-Semitism. "The vaguely articulated notions of Jewish nationalism became significant and potent when the integration of the Jews into the modern world clashed head-on with the spectre of anti-Semitism." She also said that for the Jew at the turn of the century, "a secular Jewish nationalism could be his answer to the secular nationalism which refused him entrance," and she quoted with approval Yehezkel Kaufmann's dictum that "Zionism was not born out of the fear of assimilation but out of the recognition that assimilation was impossible."

A second characteristic of the early stages of modern Zionism, according to Shapira, was its revolutionary nature. Speaking of the men and women of the second *aliyah,* she said that "their road to the modern world led through a belief in revolution, in socialism, in the remaking of society, the brotherhood of man, internationalism and utopian schemes."

Reviewing the history of Zionism, Shapira concluded her description with this question: "In which direction is Zionism moving today and what is the role which Zionism in the West can play in determining this direction?" To answer this question is, of course, to formulate Zionist ideology today.

Based on an article published in *Viewpoints* 13:3 (1984).

To start with, we must remember that Zionist ideology today is being formulated in conditions quite different from those that characterized the emergence of Zionism. For Jews today can, especially in the West, assimilate without too many obstacles. The anti-Semitism that inhibited earlier generations of "emancipated" Jews from integrating into western society is much less potent today. The principal manifestation of what remains is anti-Zionism, which suggests to some Jews that distancing oneself from Zionism improves one's chances of assimilating. Therefore, we cannot persuade our contemporaries to embrace Zionism to express themselves as modern, emancipated secular men and women; they can do so, and they do so in other ways. Affirmation of Zionism is today a firm statement against assimilation.

Similarly, we cannot fuse our children's revolutionary zeal, such as it is, with commitment to Zionism. Even if revolution means to them what it meant to the *chalutsim* of the second *aliyah*, it can no longer express itself in Zionism. For today, Zionism is perceived as particularist, elitist, bourgeois, even imperialist. Many of our children want nothing to do with it and — perhaps because they are tainted by a touch of Jewish self-hatred — they give their support to the opponents of Zionism. To them, alas, Zionism spells more often oppression than revolution.

Those who see themselves as Zionists do so not because they want to assimilate but can't, and not because they want to change the world, for assimilation is easier without Zionism, and revolution more accepted when expressed in anti-Zionist terms. Today's Zionists are committed to Judaism because Judaism today is not really possible without Zionism. Out of the despair to which western civilization has brought many of us and because of our disappointment with revolution, some of us have turned to our religious roots and found Zionism. When we wanted more of Judaism than we were given, we turned to Zionism and found our people through it.

Zionist affiliation comes to us nowadays, literally, with our synagogue membership. Whereas the membership of Diaspora Zionist political parties is decreasing, synagogue membership of religious Zionists is increasing.

Zionism, for most of us, has ceased to be a secular-revolutionary force and became a religious-bourgeois manifestation. It no longer negates our Diaspora existence. We must acknowledge this reality and actively pursue a policy of education and information in an updated version of the Zionist vision of Achad Ha'am and Martin Buber. The political response that led to the creation of the State of Israel in the land of Israel has made it possible to offer a spiritual-cultural framework for the renewal of the people of Israel and the faith of Israel. What follows is an attempt to formulate this old-new Zionism.

As I argued in chapter 2, the achievement of Zionism, that is, the establishment of the Jewish state, completed the triangle that is Israel. Until then, and for most of its history, Israel had been faith and Israel had been people. Israel as land was a dream that permeated faith and people. The reality of the land completed the triad and changed the nature of all three; it made Israel whole, and it made it different. Jewish thought is wrestling with the implications of how the faith of Israel and the people of Israel have been transformed by the possession of the land of Israel. Judaism has entered a new phase: it is not only suspended from heaven, but rooted in the soil. As a result, every conscious Jew has become something of a Zionist, and every Zionist and supporter of the land of Israel, has become involved with the people and the faith. The distinction between religionists and secularists has disappeared, despite the institutions that suggest the contrary.

The completion of the triad of Israel as faith, people and land produced a new triad. The existence of the land brought a new dimension of hope in the perception of the people of Israel in relation to the faith of Israel. Similarly, the new situation made the people relate to the land as a new category: power. And, finally, the relationship of the faith to the land expresses itself in a new struggle for righteousness. Therefore, if faith-people-land form one triangle, hope-power-righteousness form the other.

Since hope is the outcome of the encounter of faith and people, power of people and land, and justice of faith and land, this second triangle forms — with the first — the *Magen David*.

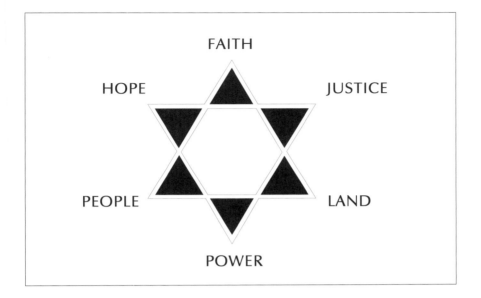

As Gershom Scholem has shown, it was Zionism that gave the *Magen David* new vitality and new meaning.[1] It may, therefore, be appropriate to plagiarize Franz Rosenzweig's *Star of Redemption* and describe the prospect of deliverance that Zionism constitutes with the same symbol. Rosenzweig's interconnecting triangles are grounded in philosophy; those that Zionism created have their roots in history; both have profound theological implications.

The emergence of Zionism and the establishment of the State of Israel have transformed Judaism in all its aspects. Therefore, it is not enough to speak of the centrality of Israel. If there was such a term, we should rather speak of the "Israelness" of Judaism, epitomized in this illustration that tries to make the *Magen David* a metaphor for contemporary Judaism and Jewishness.

The triumph of Zionism made Judaism whole, yet our task is not complete. The birth of the State of Israel may have completed the task of Zionism as far as the first triad is concerned, but it has not yet tackled the second. Therefore, we must ask ourselves: How does the existence of Israel as faith, people and land affect our understanding of hope, power and righteousness?

Attempting to point to the theological implications of the Six Day War, Eugene Borowitz, a prime exponent of liberal Judaism, wrote at the time that "to our own surprise we sensed the presence of a transcendent reality operating in history that we had almost come to believe could no longer make itself felt there."[2] That surprise had already come to many Holocaust survivors in 1948. To them, the establishment of the Jewish state was evidence that, despite everything they had been through, life was worth living. It was worth bringing children into the world and rearing them as Jews. Jews who have experienced the Holocaust see Zionism as a metaphor for hope, whether or not they live in Israel.

The establishment of the State of Israel based on faith, people and land has rooted hope in reality. That it has been "secularized" in the process has only increased its significance and, perhaps paradoxically, made it even more a function of the sacred. The redemption of the land by secular means has given hope, inherent in the impact of our faith on our people, even greater poignancy.

The connection between Holocaust and sovereignty means many things to Jews. It is the nearest we have to a guarantee that the Holocaust will not recur as long as there is a Jewish state. That is the basis of our hope. When we say that with Zionism Jews came to control their own destiny — at least to the same extent as other peoples, since we are no longer solely dependent on the actions of others for our existence — we are saying we have become actors on the arena of history. Because we are actors, rather than mere objects, what happened to us under the Nazis cannot happen again. That is the message we convey to our children and, if they don't understand it in theory, many of them feel it when they are in the land. To bring them to Israel, to visit or to settle, must, therefore, remain a crucial practical task. It is how we live out the hope of our people rooted in faith. Tourism has become a lesson in the ideology of our time.

The existence of the State of Israel is the foundation of the existence of the people and the faith, manifested in hope. Nothing that threatens that existence can, in terms of Jewish self-understanding, be morally justified. It is for Zionists to articulate this by their unconditional commitment to the state and its security — whatever government is in power. Those who established the Jewish state made hope the patrimony of the Jewish people. Those who subscribe to the ideology of Zionism regard it as their duty not to squander it.

Hope compels us to support Israel in its quest for continuity and security, whatever other objectives and objections we may have. Hope also compels us to dispel the myth of our viability in the Diaspora without Israel. But it can only be sustained by power.

The existence of Jewish power enables us to test our teachings. The State of Israel will confirm the truth of Judaism or destroy it. If the Jewish state acts like all other states in its exercise of power, it will have rendered Judaism obsolete. Therefore, inevitably, special demands are made on Israel. In the debate about whether the task of Zionism is to normalize the Jewish people or bring the messianic era closer, we cannot remain undecided but must opt for the messianic alternative. Without it, the first triangle is rendered meaningless, for it only replaces faith with land and is still not a triangle — the whole structure collapses.

How then, do we affirm power, support those who exercise it and, yet, remain true to our messianic aspirations? Or, to put it differently, how do we retain hope *and* power? As will be argued later in this book, memory is the key to our morality.

As Jews, we must accept the reality of history that brings us into the realm of power. But, as Jews, we must also remember our long history of powerlessness; if we don't, we will have denied the past, even betrayed it; if we do, we will have remained true to our heritage. The memory of the Holocaust should not be a tool in the ruthless exercise of power, but, on the contrary, a corrective to it.

This, in turn, means that our unconditional support for Israel is not identical with our unconditional support for the government of Israel. The political orientation of Israel must be a matter for the Israeli electorate. If we want a say in it, we must draw the obvious conclusion and make *aliyah*. But, as Jews, we have the right, nay the duty, to ally ourselves with those forces in Israel that appear to exercise power with the memory of powerlessness. By remaining apolitical and committed to the depoliticization of the Zionist organization, we must feel free to speak our minds on any issue that affects the *Magen David*.

For Israel is the state of the Jewish people and its life and orientation concern us all. Sometimes, our line will be identical with the policy of this or that party; sometimes it will not, for truth is not easy to label. But our criteria should be clear: we do not interfere in any way in the process that brings about a democratically elected government in Israel, whether we like the outcome or not; we *do* criticize any move by that government, or anyone, that threatens to jeopardize the Jewishness of Israel, for then we are all affected and the *Magen David* is in danger.

The necessity to support Israel as a function of hope, which in turn is the outcome of the interaction between people and faith, and the need to be critical of Israel in the light of our perception of power, as the outcome of the interaction between people and land, lead us to the consideration of righteousness as the outcome of the interaction between faith and land. If we are to support Israel unconditionally, and yet allow ourselves to be critical of those who exercise power in Israel, our guidelines must be rooted in righteousness to the land and in the land. And that quest for righteousness inevitably must lead us to consider our attitude to the Arabs.

If the hope of Israel is to remain a reality, it cannot be founded on the despair of others; if the power of Israel is to be exercised with the moral corrective of memory, other people must not be vanquished. War can only be justified if it leads to peace, not if it leads to more wars. Righteousness must be the basis on which we build our attitude and our policy to all humanity.

Working for Arab–Jewish understanding must, therefore, remain an integral part of Zionist ideology. It is an aspect that Zionism has until now neglected at enormous cost. As we affirm our support for Israel as vested in hope, we must also find ways to co-operate and understand for the sake of righteousness, otherwise the *Magen David* will be broken.

Prudent men and women will tell us that this is a noble enterprise, but an unrealistic one. For our quest for righteousness will be distorted and abused by a hostile propaganda machinery in the Arab world and in the West. Our qualifications of Jewish power will be seen as a loss of nerve to be exploited by enemies. And our affirmation of hope will be viewed as lack of loyalty to the countries in which we live. Therefore, even to utter the sentiments expressed here may be seen as opening Satan's mouth. However, we may have to take that risk and speak that which our tradition and our consciences bid us say.

How do we translate this ideological stance into practical action? Our first task is educational. It is a fallacy to assume that Jews around the world are ideologically committed to Israel and that they recognize it as essential for their future as Jews. To educate our people, young and old, to this truth is a primary responsibility. The "Israelness" of our Judaism is ignored or denied by many of our fellow Jews who still believe that lofty universalism or tepid piety is all that the Lord requires of them. To alert them to the truth, and to educate them in its implications, remains the main task of today's Zionist movement.

We must also help each other adjust to the new era in Jewish life and accept that we have the right *and* the means to shape our own future. That carries with it responsibilities but, however grave these may be, they do not entitle us to refrain from acting. If we refrain, we return to the state of powerlessness, hankering, like our ancestors in the desert, for the security — and the degradation — of slavery. To accept the reality of the new era, and to act on it, should enable us to formulate our Judaism in a new light and find a new basis for affirmation *and* criticism of Israeli policies. We must see ourselves as ardent students of Israeli political life *and* as exponents of Judaism in relation to that life. If the first task is to bring Zionism to contemporary Judaism, the second must be to bring back Judaism to Zionism.

The basis of our critique is righteousness. This means, not only righteousness and justice for Jewish minorities, but for all. As a Reform Jew and a Zionist, I would like to belong to those who spearhead a fusion between the noble principles of universalism and the lofty ideals of social action. Israel is our only opportunity to make Judaism relevant and authentic. My opposition to Israeli Orthodoxy is based on the knowledge that it has set out to block every attempt in that direction.

The new vista for Zionism may appear too grand. However, unless we opt for the grand design, we will remain in the shifting confines of inept party politics, instead of striving towards an ambitious vision for the future. And it is the future that ideology is all about.

Notes

1 Gershom Scholem, "The Star of David: History of a Symbol," in *The Messianic Idea in Judaism* (New York: Schocken, 1972).

2 Eugene B. Borowitz, "Hope Jewish and Hope Secular," *Judaism* 17:2 (Spring 1968): 145.

10

Reform Zionism in the Postmodern Age

Let us look at Jewish history in terms of the argument Thomas Kuhn articulated in *The Structure of Scientific Revolutions.*[1] Kuhn asserts that scientific advances are not made incrementally, but through dramatic shifts in the basic approach by the community of scientists. He calls them "paradigm shifts" and suggests they occur each time a different constellation of beliefs and values emerges, coupled with social and historic factors prevalent at the time.

Although Kuhn wrote about science, his theory seems to have such wide implications that it is now being applied to very diverse areas of human concerns. I feel I have been vindicated in my earlier application of this theory to the contemporary Jewish condition by the writings of Hans Kung, the distinguished and controversial Catholic theologian. Kung's most recent — and, in our context, most relevant — work, the massive volume, *Judaism,* views his subject from a theological perspective.[2] He describes the various epochs in Jewish history as paradigm shifts, cultural and religious constellations that determined how Jews saw themselves and the world at given points in time.

Kung supports the view that the penultimate paradigm shift in Jewish history coincided with the fundamental changes that took

---

This is the first part of an essay with the same title that appeared in the first issue of the *Journal of Reform Zionism* (March 1993).

place in Jewish life after the Enlightenment and the French Revolution. Out of those changes, first, Reform Judaism and, later, modern political Zionism, emerged. We are now in the midst of the latest paradigm shift, caused by the Holocaust and the creation of the State of Israel that, again, has forced Jews to view their situation from a novel, even revolutionary, perspective. As a result, Jewish history now appears in a very different light from only a generation or two ago.

Without wishing to pass judgement on Kung as a theologian and analyst of Judaism, and recognizing that his book was written out of deep sympathy for his subject and with many insights gleaned from Jewish writers, I suggest that we too attempt to describe the relationship between Reform Judaism and Zionism from the perspective of Kuhn's theory.

However, under the influence of Eugene Borowitz, instead of using the terminology of Kuhn and Kung exclusively, I will call that penultimate period in Jewish history "the age of modernity," and the current period, "the postmodern age."[3] The endeavour to formulate Reform Zionism today is very much a reflection of the struggle of Reform Judaism to move from modernity to postmodernism; from the age of Enlightenment in the aftermath of the French Revolution, to the age of Jewish sovereignty in the aftermath of the Holocaust.

One characteristic of the Enlightenment paradigm was its naively optimistic and largely secular formulation of Jewish messianism. In their belief in human reason and perfectibility, many Jews saw the dawn of a new era that would revolutionize Judaism and, simultaneously, consummate its most noble ideals of *tikkun olam,* mending the world, and making it a better place for all humanity. The Jews of western Europe and the New World, who had experienced emancipation and integration, in a spirit of great optimism shaped Reform Judaism in universalistic terms. On the other hand, those who had been moved by East European nationalism and were also severely constrained by anti-Semitism, believed that they were realists when they asserted that the new era could only be manifest to Jews in a Jewish homeland. Theirs was particularist, political Zionism.

Whereas Reform Judaism was fuelled by the messianic overtones of secular liberalism, the driving force of early Zionism was the messianism of secular socialism. The two Jewish movements had much in common, but were also very far apart. The messianic vision they shared pointed them in opposite directions. The vision of Reform Judaism was firmly rooted in the Diaspora; the vision of Zionism had its focus in the land of Israel. But as every Messiah in Judaism is, in the end, a false Messiah, it was only a matter of time before the proclamation by each side of the end of the "Jewish problem" proved to be premature. Neither the universalist nor the particularist vision has, as yet, triumphed. Both liberalism and socialism have been widely discredited in the eyes of the Jewish people and by the world.

As a result, classical-liberal Reform Judaism and political-socialist Zionism have become anachronisms. Those who cling to them impede progress. The old presuppositions are no longer current. We are now in search of a new paradigm.

The emerging new constellation of ideas and circumstances is giving birth to that paradigm. It is founded on the need to fuse universalism and particularism, not into an impossible compromise, but in a realistic dialectic. Reform Zionism is in the forefront of this struggle. It is engaged in the historic task of merging two modernist messianic visions into one programme.

Eugene Borowitz is among those who have tried to articulate it. In his latest book, *Renewing the Covenant,* he formulates the first of his "five premises for Jewish duty" of postmodern Judaism as involvement with the one God of the universe. The second he describes in this way: "A Jewish relationship with God inextricably binds selfhood and ethnicity, with its multiple ties of land, language, history, traditions, fate and faith." Then he elaborates:

> Nowhere can Jews hope to better fulfil the multilayered responsibilities enjoined on them by the covenant than in the land of Israel organized as a political, sovereign, self-determining nation, the State of Israel. Every Jewish self must face the Covenantal challenge of the desirability of moving there to join the Jewish people in working out its uniquely full response to God's demand that we sanctify social existence. Jews who do not find themselves

able to fulfil this behest must nonetheless live by a particularly intense tie to the land of Israel and measure their Diaspora fulfilment of the ethnic obligations of Jewish selfhood by the standard of the State of Israel's Covenant accomplishments.[4]

Kuhn defines paradigms as "universally recognized scientific achievements that, for a time, provide model problems and solutions to a community of practitioners."[5] Marilyn Ferguson, a follower of Kuhn who has helped popularize his theory and widen its application, put it more succinctly: "A paradigm shift is a distinctly new way of thinking about old problems."[6]

As already indicated, in contemporary Jewish history this would mean that the impact of the French Revolution and its call for liberty, equality and fraternity made Jews look at their destiny in a different way from how they saw their existence before the emancipation. Similarly, the impact of the Holocaust and the establishment of the State of Israel have again shifted the paradigm. We are now trying to adjust to that shift; the tensions within Reform Judaism reflect the tensions between the two paradigms.

Those who are "out in the field" know that it is a very painful process. In the world of what Kuhn calls normal science, adjustment to the new is usually resisted; it "often suppresses fundamental novelties because they are necessarily subversive of its basic commitments." Only when "the profession can no longer evade anomalies that subvert the existing tradition of scientific practice — then begin the extraordinary investigations that lead the profession, at last, to a new set of commitments, a new basis for the practice of science."[7]

Translated into our struggle, this means the old paradigm continues to defend itself as long as possible, despite the new situation. Only when this is not possible will the new replace the old, painfully but inescapably. Thus, even in the decades following the Holocaust and the establishment of the State of Israel, Reform Judaism continued to function as if neither event had happened. We were so in the grip of nineteenth-century liberal universalism that we failed to fathom the radical shift.

It took us more than two decades — until the Six Day War — before we realized the impossibility of the old paradigm and began to think in terms of the new. Reform Zionism is the child of that new paradigm. This does not mean, of course, that there were no Reform exponents of the new paradigm before that time. However, they were, in Ferguson's phrase, conspirators, men and women, who as individuals, advocated a certain stance, often outside, and occasionally despite, organized Reform Judaism. Reform's commitment to the new paradigm is barely two decades old and, therefore, still in a state of flux.

Nor does this, or any other, paradigm shift mean that perennial truths must be discarded. On the contrary. In Ferguson's words:

> A new paradigm involves a principle that was present all along but unknown to us. It includes the old as a partial truth, one aspect of How Things Work, while allowing for things to work in other ways as well. By its longer perspective, it transforms traditional knowledge and the stubborn new observations, reconciling their apparent contradictions.[8]

Applied to our context, this would mean the new paradigm in Jewish history restates the perennial Jewish quest for redemption; the thrust towards the messianic future, but in a new light. It evokes the love of Zion as expressed by psalmist and prophet, mystic and poet, yet speaks a different language. To repeat: it affirms the perennial truth in a novel and revolutionary way.

The modernist paradigm saw this future in universalist or nationalist terms. It was the battle between classical Reform and political Zionism. The new, postmodern, paradigm seeks to fuse the two partial truths of Jewish universalism and Jewish nationalism into something new and different. It helps us to be a little more correct than we were before and, by responding to reality as we find it, much more authentic. By rooting itself in the perennial Jewish commitment to a messianic future, the postmodern paradigm helps us find our way back to the sources and go forward towards the Promised Land.

Therefore, the first plank of a Reform Zionism platform should be the commitment to celebrate the new paradigm by adding the nationalist dimension to the universalist stance of Reform Judaism. Ferguson is as critical of the cavalier repudiation of the previous stance as she is of its dogmatic defence. The formula she advocates is along the lines of: I was partially right yesterday, and I hope that I am a little more partially right today.

There is no need or reason to denounce the noble universalist ideas and ideals of the founders of our movement, although their hopes have not been realized. That the Holocaust vindicated Jewish particularism and challenged the faith of the early Reformers, does not mean that they were wrong. Consider how they changed Jewish history for the better! They were children of their times, as we are of ours; their paradigm made sense then, as ours does now. Their shortcoming may have been linked to their neglect of the inherent tension in Judaism between the universalist and the particularist. Our commitment is to restore that tension, not to banish *ribbono shel olam,* 'the Master of the Universe,' in favour of *elohey yisrael,* 'the God of Israel.' We know the Eternal is both and infinitely more.

That is what to "Zionize" Reform Judaism means. It must not be achieved by breast-beating over past sins and by denouncing our earlier history. And it cannot be achieved by merely adding Israel to the list of philanthropies that Reform Jews support; or including Israel among the countries it is important for Jews to visit; or praising Israel's ability to integrate hapless Jewish refugees. It can never mean less than that, but if it only means that, Zionism is reduced to a vacuous idea. To "Zionize" Reform Judaism means to restore the dimension of distinctive particularist Jewish commitments and Jewish practices to the fabric of our Jewish life and our understanding of Judaism. It is to take Zionism beyond fund-raising.

If Reform Zionist organizations the world over have done nothing more than opened our eyes in this way, *dayenu,* it would have justified their existence. But they have done, and are doing, more — much more. Had our only objective been to "Zionize" Reform Judaism, we might achieve it without being involved in the World Zionist Organization (WZO). Those who have attended Zionist congresses can testify to the futility of the enterprise and to the frustration of most, if not all, of the participants. I am prepared to concede that we don't need the WZO to do our work within our movement. We will also likely receive funds for some of our programmes in Israel from the Jewish Agency even if we are not members of the WZO. But I am quite sure that the WZO needs us. Therefore, we must remain part of it, which brings me to the second plank of my proposed platform.

In the same way as universalist Reform is a noble, though insufficient, manifestation of Judaism, so is particularist-nationalist, once strongly socialist, modern Zionism. Like classical Reform, political Zionism was not wrong and was very necessary. Again, consider its historic achievements. Yet, Zionism must become "more partially right." Reform's job is to make it so, if for no other reason than that the other components of the WZO are incapable of it. That we are relative newcomers on the scene should not inhibit us in this historic undertaking.

It is a matter of great urgency. The threat of secularization of Jewish life in Israel, no less than elsewhere in the world, and the ensuing polarization into total indifference or fundamentalist obscurantism, are obstacles in the struggle for Jewish continuity. We must not be blind to the irony that the partial triumphs of Jewish universalism — the almost total integration of Jews, particularly in North America and western Europe — and Jewish nationalism — the State of Israel — also carry the seed of menacing erosion from within.

The success in integration by Jews in the western Diaspora and Israeli sovereignty have legitimized Jewish secularism. Often this manifests itself as Jewish civil religion that proclaims "horizontal transcendence." It threatens the fabric of our faith, namely our belief in God and submission to God's will. Celebrating the new paradigm must not blind us to the possibility of the paradigm being abused by most of those who call themselves Reform Jews.

By seeking to prevent the polarization of religion and secularism, or culture and religion, and by affirming that Jews are the descendants of Abraham *and* the disciples of Moses, we may help stop this most insidious form of assimilation. But we will only be heard and respected when we have solved our own problems. Unless we set particularist boundaries for Reform Judaism, its demands for greater openness in the Jewish world will be heard as calls to legitimize assimilation.

Two corollaries to this process must be mentioned in this context. Our stance must be to teach, not dictate, and we must affirm Jewish pluralism, in principle and practice. We believe there are many ways of being Jewish and many ways to find God. Let that be the third plank of our Reform Zionist platform.

However, there is a difference between the pluralism that comes from having deep convictions of one's own and respecting the deep convictions of others — true pluralism — and the pluralism that is a by-product of indifference — false pluralism. Such false pluralism is the motivation of many of our own members. How else can we explain their support for movements and organizations — Lubavitch and a host of *yeshivot,* for example — that deny them, as Reform Jews, legitimacy in the Jewish world in general, and in Israel in particular?

If the promotion of true pluralism requires sincerity in conviction and tolerance in application, its opposite is the result of religious fanaticism and political scheming. We are the victims of both. There is nothing we can do to stop religious fanaticism but we can probably do something about the political scheming. Which points to yet another plank in a possible platform: the need to depoliticize Zionism.

In this essay, I have tried to show where I come from by declaring my commitment to the theory of paradigm shifts. I have tried to say where I believe we should be going by speaking about the need to "Zionize" Reform and "sacrilize" Zionism. Earlier chapters in this book, arguing the case for linking faith, people and land, offer the theoretical foundation for this stance.

Notes

1 Thomas S. Kuhn, *The Structure of Scientific Revolutions*, 2d ed. enlarged (Chicago: University of Chicago Press, 1970).

2 Hans Kung, *Judaism: Between Yesterday and Tomorrow* (New York: Crossroad, 1992).

3 Eugene B. Borowitz, *Renewing the Covenant: A Theology for the Postmodern Jew* (Philadelphia: The Jewish Publication Society, 1991).

4 Ibid., 289–90.

5 Kuhn, viii.

6 Marilyn Ferguson, *The Aquarian Conspiracy* (London: Granada, 1982), 27.

7 Kuhn, 5–6.

8 Ferguson, 27–8.

Diaspora

Although Israel remains central to Judaism, most of the world's Jews live outside the Jewish state. The Diaspora has been an integral part of Jewry since biblical times. Its disappearance would be catastrophic, for it would endanger the universalist dimension of our tradition.

Thus, despite my affirmation of the land of Israel, reflected in the first two sections of this volume, I myself remain in the Diaspora — not to help in the holding operation while it is disintegrating, but in an effort to be among those who seek to give it vitality and purpose.

Much of my work is concerned with Jewish continuity. As a congregational rabbi, I engage in countless activities calculated to promote and preserve Jewish life from this generation to the next. Serving a Reform congregation, I seek to reach out to the marginalized and the unaffiliated in the hope of bringing them closer to the tradition and to the community. The topic of this section is the nature of that community.

The four chapters that follow reflect the argument of the Introduction — that the emphasis in Jewish life must shift from survival to continuity. The first two attempt a critical discussion of the situation in North America in general; the other two have a more specific, Canadian focus.

11

The Future of the Diaspora: An American Perspective

American Jewry is not only the largest, but also the strongest, the most resourceful, the most self-confident and the most self-sufficient part of the Jewish Diaspora. The influence of American Jewry in the Jewish world and in the United States is even larger than its numeric strength.

Yet, it is not easy to be optimistic about the future of the Diaspora, even from the North American perspective. For American Jewry is of the past and of the present; it is not of the future. What I have to say about the future of the Diaspora is, therefore, prescriptive — and, to American ears, irritatingly sermonic. Despite my great respect for American Jewry, I will not be bringing a triumphant report from the other side of the Atlantic. But before I speak of the future, let me speak of the present and the past.

I begin with the present, for the dominant force in American Jewry is the here and now. The past is often only a device that seeks to legitimize the present; it is nostalgia more than continuity. American Jewry may fantasize about the future and romanticize the past, but it lives very much in the present.

The most cogent manifestation of the present in American Jewish life is what Jonathan S. Woocher has described as "the civil religion

Paper delivered at the International Conference of the World Union for Progressive Judaism, London, May 3, 1990. Published in a somewhat different form as, "The Future of the Diaspora: A North American Perspective" in *Viewpoints* 18:2 (1990).

of American Jews." Chapter 3 lists his seven tenets of this phenomenon. They are (1) the unity of the Jewish people, (2) mutual responsibility, (3) Jewish survival in a threatening world, (4) the centrality of the State of Israel, (5) the enduring value of Jewish tradition, (6) *tzedakah:* philanthropy and social justice, and (7) Americanness as a virtue.[1] All but the fifth tenet are concerned with the present. And even it looks back to the past more with longing than with knowledge. There is nothing about the future here, for even the stress on survival looks around rather than ahead.

That is probably one reason American Jewry is so incredibly — and surprisingly — conservative. The fear of change hangs like a millstone around the neck of our largest, and ostensibly most progressive, constituent.

American Jewry is also very touchy. As I speak, I can sense hackles rise, and, no doubt, I will be told I have no right to speak of America since I am a foreigner. On the few occasions that I have ventured to be critical in public about American Jewry, even normally tolerant and urbane colleagues have been moved to react, and to persuade others whom they perceived to be more powerful, to intervene to bring me to my senses. But I am in good company.

Arthur Hertzberg, a maverick leader of American Jewry, in his history of American Jewry, has dared to be critical of his subject.[2] He questioned the past and the present and expressed doubts about the future. The reviewers were almost unanimous in their condemnation.

Those with a psychological mind-set may suggest that sensitivity to criticism depends on insecurity: a deep-seated suspicion that the criticism is legitimate, though inconvenient. I disagree: American Jewry does not wish to be criticized because it believes itself to be, deep down, approaching perfection. It sees its evolving views and practices as evidence of a new manifestation of Judaism, not only *minhag amerika,* 'American Jewish customs,' but *torat amerika,* 'American Jewish ideology,' at least as legitimate and valid as *torat eretz yisrael*, 'the Torah of Israel' perhaps even as authoritative as *torat moshe misinai*, 'Moses' Torah from Sinai.'

If this new Torah is not future-directed, that is, messianic, it is because, in its self-understanding, the future has already begun. We are said to be witnessing a kind of *atchalta digeulah,* 'the beginning of the redemptive process.' What *is* constitutes, more or less, what *ought to be*. If other Diaspora countries are different, it is usually a sign of their backwardness; the challenge is to "Americanize" world Jewry efficiently, making Americanness a universal virtue, so the family of Israel can have a *chelek ba'olam hazeh*, 'a share in this world.'

Israel may occupy a special position in this scheme of things, but it too has to see itself in the context of America. Thus American Zionists often insist that the Zionist imperative of *aliyah* does not apply to them. Sometimes one can hear American Jewish leaders speak of American Jewry, as a separate category, different from both Israel and the Diaspora.

What is this American Jewry that makes the future unnecessary? Here are some descriptions as offered by Woocher: "First, civil religion's focus and locus is in the civic and political institutions of the community, not in the conventionally religious realm."[3] He speaks of "the thoroughly insignificant role which any God-concept plays in civil religion."[4] He describes it as "a religion of horizontal transcendence" where the "lack of theological content undermines an active affirmation of vertical transcendence."[5] Woocher quotes David Elazar's description of this kind of Judaism as neo-Sadducean because "it places at the centre of its world not Torah, but the Jewish people, and makes the maintenance and expression of Jewish peoplehood its primary religious obligation."[6] The slogan "We are one," writes Woocher, "becomes a more immediate and compelling watchword of the faith" than the traditional *adonai echad*, 'the Lord is One.'[7]

How should religious Judaism that puts God in the centre and waits for God's will to be done in the fullness of time respond? Woocher lists five possible strategies and recommends the one he calls transformation. He writes: "What the strategy of transformation envisions is a civil Judaism which would outgrow the limitations of its own secular origins, and move, more overtly and securely, into the mainstream of Jewish religious tradition."[8] He names teachers who have shown us the way: Mordecai Kaplan, Martin Buber, Emil Fackenheim, Eugene Borowitz and Irving Greenberg. These men have all asserted, in Woocher's words, "that the meaning of Jewishness today lies in the return of the Jewish people to history and in the possibility of making that return a life-transforming event for the individual, the Jewish people, and perhaps even the world."[9]

Two of the five people mentioned — Borowitz, a prime exponent of liberal Judaism, and Fackenheim, a distinguished philosopher — are the thinkers of our own Reform movement, Kaplan and Buber were among our mentors and Greenberg is a friend. It is, therefore, natural to expect the strong American Reform movement to be in the forefront of this process of transformation. But it is not. In reality, it epitomizes civil religion. Instead of acting as a transforming corrective to civil religion, it acts as its most effective institutional manifestation. It has adapted the strategy Woocher calls integration, which means it has identified with civil religion. Moreover, Reform is strongly institutional with only vague and unsatisfactory attempts at stressing personal piety and observance. It is, therefore, much more powerful in its emphasis on the Jewish people than it is on Torah or God; it is — surprisingly and alarmingly — more Sadducean than Pharisaic.[10]

Since the emotional impact cannot come from the institutional strength of civil religion, it is being augmented by the past, not by a messianic future. A most potent allusion to the past is the Holocaust. Fackenheim is known in the Jewish world not because he is a distinguished philosopher but because he speaks about the Holocaust. The Holocaust evokes the Judaism of people over the Judaism of Torah and God. Therefore, the adherents of civil religion like it. It provides the framework for the myth of destruction and redemption.

The past is a cause that American Judaism has come to espouse. But causes, as Hertzberg suggests, are no substitutes for meaning, and it is meaning — which always points to the future — that this essay is about. We must heed Hertzberg's observation that "a community cannot survive on what it remembers; it will persist only because of what it affirms and believes."[11] That is why it is difficult to be very optimistic about the future of the Diaspora.

The idea of the uniqueness of the Jewish people, the foundation of civil religion, becomes meaningless without the traditional religious dimension. Hertzberg writes: "An ethnic group cannot assert 'chosenness' without falling into chauvinism or worse. In a democratic society, only a religion dares use this term and only to describe believers who are committed to live spiritual lives."[12] Unless we shift from a neo-Sadducean to a neo-Pharisaic form of Judaism, we will have nothing to say about the future.

The prefix "neo" suggests that the contemporary world must not be ignored. Israel, for example, is the most important part of that world and we must not be blind to the implications of this reality, not only for politics and institutions but for theology. Jewish sovereignty is central to the Judaism of tomorrow, in the Diaspora no less than in Israel. The State of Israel has replaced *halachah*, Jewish law, as the force that binds the faith of Israel, the people of Israel and the land of Israel into an indivisible unit. The future of Judaism is Pharisaic in the sense that God and the responsibility, *letakken olam bemalchut shaddai*, 'to help to set the world right by the rule of God,' must remain in the forefront of our Judaism. We must live with the tension between particularism and universalism if we are to continue as a viable Diaspora.

Orthodoxy, by its orientation, is unlikely to free itself from the past to meet the challenges of the future. Reform Judaism can; whether it will is another matter. It may become yet another neo-Sadducean sect of civil religion, or the normative — Pharisaic — Judaism of tomorrow. The former is something of a nightmare, the latter a historic opportunity.

To take the opportunity, we have to go easy on sociology and anthropology in favour of theology. We cannot remain merely descriptive about *minhag amerika*, but must dare be prescriptive in the spirit of Torah. Study, home observance and prayer must come before "Jewish culture," fund-raising and Holocaust commemoration — not *instead of* these, but *before* them. Civil Judaism should not be replaced, only transformed, if it is to bring us into the next century.

This means that institutional religion must be augmented with personal piety, and collective manifestations of allegiance underwritten by individual expressions of fidelity. Jewish *belonging* must be substantiated through Jewish *living*. To make that possible, standards must be set and obligations formulated — a Pharisaic phenomenon.

The potential normative Judaism of tomorrow — which centres not only on people but also on God, and which understands Torah as an expression of the divine will that points to the future, not merely as a manifestation of Jewish folk memory — cannot, therefore, be narrowly sectarian. That it stresses individual commitment before collective allegiance means that it will cut across existing denominational lines and force us to make common cause with other movements, notably with Conservative Judaism. Surely our insistence on outreach cannot only be directed towards the marginal Jews who marry non-Jewish spouses. It must include other Jews who think like us but, for one reason or another, find themselves in another cluster of synagogues.

We must also reach out to those who affirm Israel, be it on religious or so-called secular grounds, and see in Zionism the other modern messianic force, beside Reform Judaism. The fusion between Zionism and Reform — which has already begun on an institutional and political level, but which yet has to be reflected in transforming Jewish theology and thus leading us into the next century — is a prerequisite for averting the danger of sectarianism.

Here is where the World Union for Progressive Judaism has its most important ideological task. It is the only forum that brings together American Reform Judaism with the rest of the community of Progressive Judaism and puts Israel in the centre. Numerically and financially, the imbalance is tremendous in favour of America, but not ideologically.

Progressive Judaism in Israel, Europe, Australia, South Africa and Latin America is much closer to Conservative Judaism and to Zionism and much less a manifestation of civil Judaism. Because Progressive Judaism in these countries is forced to encounter Orthodoxy in its imprisonment in the past — and to battle its collusion with Jewish secularism, particularly in Israel — it is compelled to be much more open to the future. What it loses in institutional strength, it often gains in messianic vision. A collaboration with American civil religion could be a tremendous benefit to all and a formula that could make us the normative Judaism of the next century.

Notes

1 Jonathan S. Woocher, *Sacred Survival: The Civil Religion of American Jews* (Bloomington and Indianapolis: Indiana University Press, 1986).

2 Arthur Hertzberg, *The Jews in America* (New York: Simon and Schuster, 1989).

3 Woocher, 16.

4 Ibid., 91.

5 Ibid., 93.

6 Ibid., 159.

7 Ibid., 163.

8 Ibid., 171.

9 Ibid., 174.

10 Sadducees and Pharisees were the two main parties in Palestine in the period before the destruction of the Second Temple in 70 C.E. The former advocated a conservative, "priestly" stance; the latter represented a more radical, "prophetic" approach to tradition. The Pharisees came to shape Judaism as we know it today; the Sadducees are only of historic interest. The hostile and polemic depiction of Pharisaic Judaism in early Christian literature has been proven totally unwarranted by contemporary scholars of all faiths.

11 Hertzberg, 386.

12 Ibid., 387.

12

Jewish Unity:
A Challenge to
Conservative Judaism

My qualifications to speak on the subject of Jewish unity are not institutional or theological but biographical: I was born into a secular but intensely Jewish family in Poland. As a result, Jewish secularism is neither alien nor abhorrent to me, and familiarity with East European Orthodoxy has freed me from romantic notions about it. I grew up in Sweden in two congregations that were liberal but described themselves as Conservative. For a quarter of a century, I was associated with the British Reform movement, which shows affinity to Conservative and Reform Judaism in North America. Since 1983, I have been the rabbi of Holy Blossom Temple in Toronto, which though one of the pillars of the Union of American Hebrew Congregations, nevertheless is regarded as being on the Conservative end of the Reform spectrum.

I am always happier on the edge than in the centre, because I do not believe that any group in contemporary Jewry expresses the whole truth about God, Israel, Torah and the messianic future. Whatever our affiliation, we must learn from others and scrutinize ourselves. I am proud to be an activist within the Reform movement,

Address at a plenary session of the convention of the United Synagogue of America, Toronto, November 6, 1989.

not because I consider it perfect, but because I find myself less maladjusted there than I think I would be elsewhere.

My first point in the search for Jewish unity is a plea for pluralism in contemporary Jewish life. Even if the leaders of each movement believe that they, and they alone, have all the answers to our Jewish problems, they should accept and learn to live with the fact that the other movements, however misguided and objectionable they may seem, are here to stay. The earlier prognoses about the imminent demise of Orthodoxy proved to be false; the dire predictions about Reform becoming a sect on the periphery of *kelal Yisrael*, 'the Jewish people,' were equally unwarranted; unfounded also were the analyses that suggested that the Conservative movement would soon break up; and so was the idea that Reconstructionism would not survive its founder. Since pluralism is here to stay, let us not waste our energies on ideological battles and institutional rivalries. Let us instead learn to live with each other — even if, from time to time, we have to grit our teeth in the process.

So far, we have tended to confine co-operation to so-called non-religious issues: supporting Israel, fighting anti-Semitism, championing Jewish rights near and far and so on. Simultaneously, we have competed for the souls of individuals and the status of our organizations in matters religious. That kind of division does not serve the Jewish world well; the realities of Jewish life today demand that we respect each other and work together consistently in all areas.

The issue that dramatically combines almost all the others is, of course, the question of Jewish status, seen most recently in the battles to amend Israel's Law of Return. If there ever was a case for open, consistent and full co-operation between the Conservative, modern Orthodox, Reconstructionist and Reform movements, this is it. If non-Orthodox Jews will be disenfranchised in Israel, not only by the Orthodox rabbinate, as is now the case, but also by the Jewish state, the breach between Israel and the Diaspora will become a distinct possibility with catastrophic consequences for the Jewish people as a whole.

The easiest solution would be — and here I am unashamedly partisan — the one adopted by Reform rabbis the world over.

Recognize the documents of conversion and divorce issued by other rabbis, ordained by recognized authorities within each movement. This is pluralism at its purest. I am convinced that were this in operation today, the vast majority of Reform rabbis would not perform second marriages without halachically acceptable divorce documents. They might even re-think their support for patrilineality.

However, such universal and mutual acceptance is beyond our grasp. Even if Conservative rabbis would agree, Orthodox rabbis will not. And because Orthodox rabbis will not, Conservative rabbis are less likely to. I say this not to castigate the spiritual leaders of Orthodox Judaism, for I recognize that it is the nature of liberal Judaism — to which Reform and Conservative Judaism adhere — to be pluralistic, and in the nature of Orthodox Judaism to be monolithic. My aim is to seek other solutions, potentially acceptable to all concerned.

This brings me to the question of establishing joint *Batei Din,* religious courts of law, not nationally, where agreement is even less likely, for the larger the constituency the more difficult it is to reach a consensus. I mean locally, where the potential for co-operation exists, although the will is not yet there. I have spoken about this for at least 15 years, with little success. I am, however, convinced that this is the way to go; and I am not alone in this view.

Shlomo Riskin is an exponent of modern Orthodoxy, first in New York and now as Dean of Ohr Torah Institutions in Efrat on the West Bank. This Orthodox Rabbi, familiar with American and Israeli Jewry wrote in *The Jerusalem Post,* January 4, 1989:

> The hour has arrived to declare a cease-fire. Hitler sent Jews to the gas chambers irrespective of Orthodox, Conservative, Reform or secular labels. We must find a definition for 'Who is a Jew' which will embrace the largest possible number of Jews without compromising the halachic requirement. The time has come to emphasize what unites us, rather than what divides us.

Riskin's solution is simple: "I suggest the formation of Unity *Beit Din* comprising three Orthodox rabbis and an equal number of

Conservative, Reform and Reconstructionist rabbis. This council on conversion would establish, by unanimous vote, a handbook of basic Judaism, listing the fundamental laws of the holy days, *kashrut,* ethical behaviour and areas of Jewish practice vital to serious Jewish living." Since a *Beit Din* always requires at least three judges, the presence of three Orthodox rabbis could make such a court acceptable to Orthodoxy. Yet it could still involve non-Orthodox rabbis without compromising their pluralistic stance. Riskin continues:

> They might also insist on knowledge of Jewish history, at least a reading knowledge of the Hebrew language and a strong identification with the State of Israel. The understanding of this basic Judaism, a general acceptance of commandments, ritual immersion, and circumcision for men, would establish proper conversion acceptance to all branches of Judaism.

If the proposal, this time formulated by Riskin but available in many other versions, should be adopted, each side would have to pay a price. Orthodoxy would have to recognize the legitimacy of other expressions of religious Judaism. And exponents of non-Orthodox Judaism would have to limit their sovereignty and show discipline, which so far has not always come easily to them. Since neither side is likely to yield totally, a compromise as described by Riskin seems inescapable.

Reform Judaism in Canada, largely concentrated in Toronto, would probably be very receptive to such a proposal. The question is whether other groups will explore the matter. As difficult as it might be to set up a universal *Beit Din,* local *Batei Din* are possible, and Toronto is a prime candidate for such a court.

And now for the anti-climax: to date, I can report no progress at all. Every attempt to move closer has failed. What follows are some illustrations of frustration and dismay.

Soon after I came to Toronto, a person with standing in the Orthodox community in the city asked if I wanted to meet a leading Orthodox rabbi. Of course, I agreed. Several months went by and finally word came back: the rabbi had considered the matter carefully and decided against a meeting by appointment, but he would view favourably a meeting by chance. When time permits, I intend to devote a couple of weeks walking around my distinguished colleague's synagogue in the hope of getting the chance to greet him.

Meanwhile, he and his colleagues continue to preach personal attacks on Reform from their pulpits. Orthodox rabbis, except those employed by communal organizations or Conservative synagogues, boycott the Toronto Board of Rabbis. Recently, they took steps to bar non-Orthodox Jews from the *mikveh* originally built for the entire community.

The *mikveh* incident brought an unexpected benefit: Conservative and Reform rabbis were forced to co-operate to build a new *mikveh* for their use. However, a recent initiative to establish a Conservative-Reform *Beit Din* in Toronto was rejected by local Conservative rabbis. This, despite the fact that Reform conversion procedures are virtually identical with Conservative ones, and notwithstanding the desire by most Toronto Reform rabbis to have uniform divorce procedures. If we are, indeed, serious about unity with Orthodoxy, surely we should begin with ourselves!

Since, no doubt, someone is going to raise the decision of the Reform movement to accept patrilineal descent as the obstacle to halachic co-operation between Conservative and Reform Jews, let me anticipate at least some discussion.

To start with, the Reform rabbis in Toronto do not agree with the decision on patrilineality. Secondly, they would have a very strong argument in their efforts to persuade their Reform colleagues elsewhere to reverse the majority decision in favour of patrilineality, if they could vindicate their traditionalist stance by pointing to a Reform-Conservative *Beit Din*. Rebuffs by other groups only strengthen the hands of the extremist elements in my own movement. A curious collusion exists between the right of one movement and the left of the other, while those in the middle lose each time.

This suggests, therefore, that the first step towards creating a joint *Beit Din* with the Orthodox would be for Conservative, Reform and Reconstructionist Jews to come together. If the Conservative movement wants to keep its role as a catalyst, it can take some immediate initiatives by urging its constituents to engage in more tangible co-operation.

Even if Conservative Jews see themselves as being closer to Orthodox Judaism in some areas of Jewish practice, they should bear in mind that historically, sociologically and theologically they are part of the non-Orthodox camp. The Orthodox know this; hence their persistent refusal to grant concessions to Conservative Judaism in Israel. If the Orthodox establishment is to bend, it will only be out of political expediency. And such expediency can only come about when the non-Orthodox world is united in the areas that matter most in this context, namely, the granting of Jewish status. Therefore, to come closer to our Orthodox brothers and sisters, we first have to come closer to each other and thus confront Orthodoxy. Paradoxically, purposeful confrontation must precede peaceful co-existence.

In another article in *The Jerusalem Post*, June 7, 1989, Member of Knesset, Yoash Tsiddon-Chatto says:

> Some years ago, I was invited to a luncheon in Johannesburg, South Africa. There were two or three other Israelis, one of whom was Eliahu Lankin, then ambassador to Pretoria. "How is it," asked one of those present, "that you, a Palmachnik who sailed on illegal Haganah ships, agree to sit at the same table with the commander of the (Irgun ship) *Altalena,* Mr. Lankin?" I snapped back instinctively: "Sir," I said, "please note that both of us sailed the same sea, under the same flag, to the same destination."

Tsiddon-Chatto adds: "So, in my humble opinion, do the Reform Jews, and the Conservatives for that matter." We are, indeed, all in the same sea desperately trying to reach the same shores of Jewish survival and Jewish continuity. We must recognize that we should be in the same boat to reach our common destination. And instead of always telling others what they should be doing about it, let us explore what we can do, not in some distant future and in an unspecified place, but here and now.

13

London to Toronto:
Personal Impressions

When we came to Canada people were talking about a new book called *None Is Too Many*.[1] It is an account by two Jewish historians, Irving Abella and Harold Troper, of Canadian immigration policy towards Jews between 1933 and 1948. Its conclusions are epitomized by the title. Canada's politicians wanted to keep the Jews out of their country at a time when the Jews desperately needed somewhere to go. Many reasons were given for delays and cancellations of permits, but now — under the scrutiny of painstaking research — the truth could be told. It was anti-Semitism; when it came to Jews, even none was too many.

The findings were startling, but not unique to Canada. After all, Bernard Wasserstein had told a similar story in his *Britain and the Jews of Europe 1939 to 1945*.[2] Yet the latter had not stirred Anglo-Jewry the way *None Is Too Many* had upset Canadians.

The difference in reception, between essentially similar documentation on the two sides of the Atlantic, is significant. Jews in Europe take anti-Semitism for granted and, largely, learn to adapt to it. Some even believe that too much protest is counter-productive. North American Jewry is shocked each time it finds

Reprinted from *Listening to American Jews: Sh'ma 1970–1985*, ed. Carolyn Toll Oppenheimer (Port Washington, N.Y: Sh'ma, 1986), 199–201. Originally published in *Sh'ma* in 1984.

evidence of anti-Semitism and often overreacts. They are determined to make sure that what happened in the 1930s and 1940s does not happen again.

For the same reasons, support for Israel is stronger in Canada than in Britain. In fact, it is less than prudent here to express any criticism of Israeli government policies, even if they affect the lives of Diaspora Jews. The argument is that Israel has so many enemies who constantly bombard her politically and militarily that she is entitled to unquestioned and uncritical loyalty from her friends.

But this kind of friendship is superficial. Thus, although vocal and fiscal support for Israel is stronger in Canada than it is in Britain, proportionately more British Jews make *aliyah*. Canadian Jews treat Israel as a symbol, and perhaps as an insurance policy, but regard Canada as home. That is why they are so uncritical of Israel and so sensitive to anti-Semitism at home.

Yet, Canadian Jews, for all their success in business, political and public life, are not rooted in Canadian society. True, it is not easy to define Canadian identity in the way one can decide what it means to be integrated in British society. But, even allowing for that, it is remarkable how ghettoized Canadian Jews are. It makes British Jews seem integrated and at ease by comparison.

British Jews who are more integrated than others, usually leave the Jewish community altogether. In Canada, almost the opposite occurs. Apart from the Orthodox, those who belong to synagogues are often more assimilated than those who do not. For example, in Canada Holocaust survivors rarely join congregations; synagogue affiliation is too alien to them.

Their children are different. They feel more at home with North American middle-class Jewry, and synagogue affiliation is part of that. Since Reform is much more the Jewish establishment here than in Britain, those who seek their way in, join Reform congregations. The young tend to be more self-confident and mature than their parents.

That Reform is part of the Jewish establishment means that many of Canada's communal leaders belong to Reform congregations. I sat at the dinner table of a distinguished Canadian Jewish leader, who is a member of his local Reform congregation. Opposite me

was a distinguished Anglo-Jewish leader, probably no more observant than our host, but a member of an Orthodox congregation in
Britain. I asked him if he could have attained the position he had in
Anglo-Jewry, had he joined his local Reform synagogue. He didn't
think so. Neither do I.

A Reform rabbi in Canada, Dr. W. Gunther Plaut, served as
President of the Canadian Jewish Congress. No rabbi, let alone a
Reform one, could ever become President of the Board of Deputies
of British Jews.

Anglo-Jewry is undoubtedly more observant, more to the "right,"
than Canadian Jewry, but it is not more Jewish. There are probably
more kosher butchers in Britain per Jewish-population unit than in
Canada. But there are more good Jewish bookshops in Canada. The
standard of Jewish knowledge is higher in Canada, although synagogue affiliation is not. Jewish communal institutions have a high
profile in Canada and are hives of activity, but many are open on
Shabbat and serve nonkosher food.

If Golders Green, a "Jewish" area of London, has aspirations to
be the Jerusalem of Europe, then Toronto is probably more anxious
to be the Tel Aviv of North America — and it has the money and
the vulgarity to pull it off. It also has almost enough Israelis
to populate it.

The difference in outlook is also reflected in synagogue life. One
of my major challenges is to fight secularism within the synagogue.
This secularization expresses itself in scarcity of prayer and observance and in a surfeit of aesthetics and traditional rituals. As a result,
in some areas, Reform is curiously to the "left," and in others,
remarkably "right." It is less religiously observant than in Britain, but
much more "gut-Jewish." My sense of spiritual alienation is amply
compensated for by a sense of being with my people as I knew them
in Poland and Russia.

A group in my congregation had a discussion recently about
which of the two "traditional" roles of the rabbi was more in keeping
with the needs of the times: that of administrator and public
relations person or that of pastor. When I suggested that, since we
were so concerned with tradition, we should start with the rabbi as
teacher, I dropped something of a bombshell. Only a few of these

leaders had even thought of the rabbi in this way. In many congregations, the teaching is done by lesser lights or "visiting scholars." In Europe, you still expect the rabbi to be the teacher and scholar, whether he is Orthodox or liberal.

The rabbis in North America are confined to their priestly duties, which are curiously secular or, at least, intended for secular people. When I declared my intention to follow another pattern, it caused some consternation. Would he want us to be religious? Isn't it enough that he has status and position? People want to enjoy their Jewishness gastronomically and their Judaism vicariously.

But my stance has also evoked enthusiasm. People had forgotten you could be Reform and remain within the traditional orbit of learning and prayer; that it was not enough to pay lip-service to folkways and pay cash to fund-raisers. I am greatly encouraged by the response from the leadership and there are indications that some of those on the periphery might wish to join. Whether the existing institutional structure will tolerate it, remains to be seen. I am full of hope that my European habits will bear some fruit.

The challenge is twofold: to establish a different style of rabbinate and to equip the institution to tolerate the change. The former is easier. Individuals are receptive to new ideas, whereas organizations are not. But it is also a test for Reform: if it is true to itself, it must allow change and it must fight rigidity and secularism in its own circles with at least the same vehemence that it fights it in Orthodoxy. I see myself as an emissary from the Old World in this struggle. I wonder how the institutional machinery of the new one will respond.

Happily, there is no reason to fight Orthodoxy, for this is a tolerant community. That Reform was on the scene first, that it is part of the establishment and that many, if not most, of the communal leaders belong to Reform or Conservative congregations, makes it impossible for Orthodoxy to have its way as it has in Britain and in Europe. But with an increasing radicalization of Orthodoxy, and the ascendance of extreme elements all over the world, things may change for the worse in Canada, too.

Meanwhile, Toronto appears as a haven of tolerance. The mother of a leader of my congregation died recently. A leading Orthodox rabbi attended the service in the synagogue (Reform and

Conservative congregations often hold funeral services in synagogues in Canada). Before the service, the same rabbi came to see me in my study to welcome me to Toronto. I cannot imagine any of the *dayanim* of the Orthodox London *Beit Din* doing the same.

When I was a child in Poland, I was often asked whom I loved best, my father or my mother. As a middle-aged rabbi in Canada, I am often asked if I prefer London to Toronto. The question of today baffles me as much as the question from my childhood used to perplex me.

Comparative evaluation is impossible. Who I am today has been shaped by the Leo Baeck College in London, the Reform Synagogues of Great Britain and the two London congregations I served for 21 years. But I also know that what I have been doing since my arrival in Toronto has been exciting and rewarding. The vitality of American Jewry is infectious.

There used to be an advertisement in New York: "Dress British — Think Yiddish!" I try to live by it. But I have now acquired another motto: "Feel British — Act Canadian!" It is, as Americans say, a meaningful and enriching experience.

Notes

1 Irving Abella and Harold Troper, *None Is Too Many* (Toronto: Lester & Orpen Dennys, 1983).

2 Bernard Wasserstein, *Britain and the Jews of Europe 1939 to 1945* (Oxford: Clarendon Press, 1979).

14

Is There a Future for Canadian Jewry?

Jewish history provides ample evidence that no Jewish community, however numerous and prosperous, has an assured future. And no Jewish community, however small and exposed, is destined for extinction. In my lifetime, I have seen the large and flourishing Jewish community in my native Poland disappear. I have also seen the small and struggling community of Sweden, where I grew up, persevere against all odds.

Therefore, it would be foolish to answer "Yes" or "No" to the question before us. The future of Canadian Jewry is not secure or precarious. It is, like the future of Diaspora Jewry, uncertain. All we can do is try to assess the prospects of our survival.

We begin by reflecting on the total dependence of Canadian Jewry on Jewish life in the United States. Although we may often say that Canadian Jewry is better than American Jewry, little suggests that it is very different. Canadian Jews see themselves as closer to tradition and less prone to the excesses of Jewish life elsewhere. But this may be more a sign of provincialism than of superiority. The "ours-is-better" syndrome is often a manifestation of insecurity, not the outcome of an objective assessment.

From the viewpoint of structure and allegiance, every Canadian synagogue of significance is a constituent of an American organization.

Contribution to a symposium with the same title, *Viewpoints* 19:3 (1991).

Most of the rabbis in Canada were not only trained in the United States but are American citizens.

Except for *Viewpoints,* Canadian Jewry has no serious Jewish journal. And it is not known for its specific contribution to Jewish scholarship. Jewish scholarly creativity in Canada is almost invariably an offshoot of the American mainstream; most teachers of Jewish studies in Canadian universities have probably been trained in the United States.

The praise that Canadian Jewry deservedly receives is for doing the same things American Jewry does — but better. We raise more money per capita for the United Jewish Appeal, more of our children go to Jewish day schools and a higher percentage of the community belong to congregations. Our uniqueness, therefore, is paradoxically, most in evidence in our conformity, which may be a very Canadian trait, indeed.

Since, by all accounts, American Jewry is the most likely Diaspora community to survive, there is every reason to believe that the future of Canadian Jewry is reasonably certain. However, even American Jewry is in danger due to its lack of a vision of the future; it is too firmly rooted in the present and too anxious to remain unchanged. Again, what is true of the United States is even more true of Canada.

There are other dangers. The historian of Zionism, David Vital, points to a serious threat to the survival of the Diaspora in general, and the American Diaspora in particular. In *The Future of the Jews,* he suggests that Jews in the Diaspora can only affiliate as individuals and, therefore, opt out when expedient. Jews in Israel, by contrast, are part of a collective under the jurisdiction of the Jewish state. They can only opt out by emigration, not by ceasing to pay dues to synagogues or by withdrawing their children from religious schools.[1]

A community that depends on voluntary association is always vulnerable, for it is subject to economic and political shifts. Thus, each time the country suffers a recession, Jewish institutions are at risk; our Jewishness is too often linked to the cost of living index.

Economic dependence, rather than a passion for Torah, makes the man or woman of means, not the scholar, the leader of the community. In fact, "to show leadership" has become the most common euphemism for giving a lot of money. As we see wealth being gained and lost with frightening speed, we should worry about the future of our community.

Yet, this is not a plea to reinstate rabbis as the leaders of Diaspora Jewry. We do not deserve it. For the future of Jewry has never depended on bookish learning; at best, only the past has been preserved in this way. The future depends on vision, and rabbis do not seem to have more of it than others. They, too, have fallen prey to the all-pervasive conservatism of our time.

The most visible manifestation of passion in Canadian Jewry is linked to our concern for Israel. That is not surprising because you cannot motivate many individuals; you can only motivate a collective, and only Israel speaks the language of the collective.

Paradoxically, most Jewish leaders try to safeguard the future of their communities in the Diaspora by appealing to loyalty to Israel. Simultaneously, and neurotically, they fall short of drawing the obvious conclusions and advocating *aliyah*. We realize we are more likely to remain Jews if we rally around Israel, but we do not want to take the consequences and live in Israel. Our individualism, which enables us to flourish in the Diaspora as a people, gets the better of us, and we must accept it.

But soon we may have to choose to live in a non-Jewish environment that only allows us to be Jewish by choice, and, therefore, tempts us to assimilate, or see ourselves as part of the Jewish polity that is Israel. This need not mean that we should live permanently in Israel. But it does mean that we should recognize the Jewish state as the place of the Jewish people, even if the space of Jewish individuals and groups may be elsewhere. We may all have to adopt the mentality of *yordim*, men and women who have left Israel "only for a limited time."

Linking ourselves to Israel in this way goes far beyond financial contributions. It must mean cultural commitment and spiritual allegiance. As long as the Jewish state is strong and viable — not only militarily but Jewishly — Jewish communities that acknowledge their bond to Israel will flourish. It would then truly become the state of the Jewish people, not only of its citizens. Without that bond, our future seems problematic. The declining numbers, due to low birth rate and intermarriage, coupled with growing economic uncertainty that will continue to plague us, may mean that soon we will not even be able to afford to maintain our own institutions.

But what about religious commitment? Will not fidelity to God and Torah guarantee our survival? I yearn to answer with a resounding Yes. However, I am bound to concede that religious commitment in our time can only address itself to individuals; there will always be a "saving remnant," large or small.

But to ensure that the community continues to flourish, collective steps must be taken — and it is these that are most problematic in the Diaspora. That is why we need the "vicarious" collectivism that Israel stimulates.

The future is not only subject to forces beyond our control; it is also in our hands. Therefore, if we wish to assure a future for Canadian Jewry, besides our religious practices, we must promote activities that will link us to the Jewish people. That link is inconceivable without making Israel central to our communal concerns.

Note

1 David Vital, *The Future of the Jews* (Cambridge, Mass.: Harvard University Press, 1990).

Action

One of the arguments in this book is that *halachah,* Jewish law, has ceased to be operative in Jewish life. *Mitzvot,* commandments that Jews, as individuals, voluntarily take upon themselves, are the actions by which we primarily manifest our allegiance to God.

As modernists, we know such actions cannot be confined to rituals. As proud citizens of the countries in which we live, we also know that the freedom and opportunities of Diaspora existence have brought new responsibilities for the Jewish people. Many of these can be placed under the rubric of *tikkun olam,* the traditional Jewish imperative to 'mend the world.' We are called upon to be in the forefront of social action.

And then there is the memory of the six million. Having experienced the Holocaust, it behooves us to seek to prevent potential holocausts everywhere. Having moved from the almost-exclusive preoccupation with survival to the concern for continuity, we are being called upon to manifest it in solidarity with all who suffer.

That is the theme of Chapter 15. The two chapters that follow are variations on it, one dealing specifically with the Reform perspective, which is the particular bias of this book, the other with the situation in Canada.

15

Silence — Survival — Solidarity

I became aware of the Holocaust when I was eight or nine years old and listened to the news coming through the only radio in the *kolchoz* (collective farm) in Uzbekistan, where my parents and I spent most of the war years. As the Red Army spokesperson reported on the extermination camps and the millions of dead, the adults around me almost invariably concluded that it could not possibly be like that; it must be Soviet propaganda to fuel hatred against the German enemy. Even if, during the year between the end of the war and our return to our native Poland, we had not heard from any of our relatives, my parents, like many others who were with us, still believed that the family, if not intact, would at least still number many and would be waiting for us when we returned. When the truth finally dawned on them, they were silent. It was an awesome silence.

I think of it whenever I recall Aaron's silence upon hearing that two of his sons had been devoured by the "strange fire" they offered up in the sanctuary (Leviticus 10:3). But in the biblical tale, at least, Aaron's silence is explained. We knew of no reason for what we found; our silence was not the result of self-control, but came out of an inability to utter words when confronted with the truth of the fires of the crematoria.

Those who survived the camps were also unable to speak. When, a couple of years after our return to Poland, we emigrated to Sweden

Reprinted from *Elie Wiesel: Between Memory and Hope*, ed. Carol Rittner (New York: New York University Press, 1990).

and lived with many of those who had been rescued by the Swedish Red Cross in the final days of the war, I was again struck by the silence. The survivors spoke among themselves, but not to outsiders, because "they" would not understand. When people would hear of the horrors of the camps, some Swedes, including Jews, would say to survivors that things hadn't been that easy in Sweden either. After all, shoes had been rationed during the war. One former camp inmate was actually asked by a fellow Jew who had been spared the ordeal if it had been very difficult to obtain kosher food. In the face of such questions and such reactions, what else could there be but silence?

Jan Karski, courier between the Polish underground and the Allies, attempted to alert the free world to the plight of the Jews by giving an eyewitness account of what was happening in the Warsaw ghetto. Prominent American leaders declared that they found it impossible to believe him. If they found it impossible, what could one expect from ordinary folk, including ordinary Germans? In the 1960s, a German pastor, Dieter Schoeneich, and I had initiated a reconciliation programme between Protestant youths in Germany, all born after 1945, and Jews in Britain, where I was working at the time. There were not enough Jews in Germany for that kind of programme. One recurring question Jewish hosts asked their German visitors was, "What did your parents know?" Perhaps the parents knew much but would not admit it because of the amnesia that comes from guilt. But perhaps they did not know, in the way others did not know, and in the way those Jews listening to the radio in a remote Uzbekistan *kolchoz* did not know. In the face of such ignorance, silence seemed inescapable. Every attempt at language failed because it sought to express the unthinkable.

Language also failed because, ultimately, language itself had been debased. That is a central theme in the writings of George Steiner. He explains this attack on the German language by declaring, "I believe that the matter of the relations between language and political inhumanity is a crucial one; and . . . I believe that it can be seen with specific tragic urgency in respect of the uses of German in the Nazi period and in the acrobatics of oblivion which followed on the fall of Nazism."[1]

Disbelief did not only come to those who mourned the victims, or to those who descended from the perpetrators; sometimes it affected the victims themselves. In an exchange between Emil Fackenheim, theologian of the Holocaust par excellence, and Elie Wiesel, its best-known witness, at a symposium on Jewish values in the post-Holocaust future, the latter recalled a question he was asked about whether he really believed what had happened to him. Wiesel: "Well, Emil, I do not believe it. The event seems unreal, as if it occurred on a different planet."[2] That is, incidentally, one reason revisionism, invariably vicious and malicious, is so painful to the survivors. It abuses their silence.

Yet, in the face of such disbelief, silence remains the only humanly possible response. Wiesel's concluding words in his opening statement at the same symposium — "That is the problem, that is my fear: perhaps whatever we try to write and say about Jewish values and Jewish experience has no relationship to either"[3] — prompted the chairperson of the event to summarize the contribution of the other participants — besides Wiesel and Fackenheim, George Steiner and Richard H. Popkin — as "we pretty much agree that the ultimate reaction is silence."[4]

Silence may have been inevitable, but it was also unbearable. That is why, paradoxically, survivors had to speak and write, if for nobody else than for themselves: to make themselves believe the truth. Even if they could not speak to outsiders, perhaps they could speak to each other. And they did. I spent my adolescent years in the company of camp survivors. I do not remember them talking of much else. They told of their experiences repeatedly; it was necessary for their existence, their survival. They recalled death and suffering so they could live.

The late Dr. Shammai Davidson's research on the survivor syndrome is significant. Comparing groups of survivors in Israel and California, he found that, although the latter were much more affluent and successful, the former seemed happier. He concluded that this was because survivors living in California found it difficult to speak of what had happened to them in the camps, because the cultural milieu was not conducive to such testimony. But it was proper and easy to speak in Israel, because the culture encouraged the talking and sharing. Silence may have been expedient in one's business dealings in the New World, but, apparently, dangerous for one's mental well-being. Similarly, parents who wanted to spare their children born after the war their gruesome experiences caused them more anguish than those who shared with the young the truth, and thus could go on together like Abraham and Isaac on their way down from Moriah.

This explains the centrality of Y' Vashem and all the other monuments in Israeli public life. They are national shrines designed to honour the memory of the martyrs and provide survivors with opportunities to grieve together. They also make it possible to break the silence and survive. Although many of those who have spoken and written, insist that they recognize in their speaking the purpose of why they survived, it may be legitimate to put it differently. They did not survive to speak, they spoke to survive. Even if nobody "out there" wants to listen, survivors must speak to live. Thus the paradox of speaking and writing about silence: uttering words to prove that nothing can be said.

When speaking and writing is no longer possible, there seems little point in going on. Is that why Paul Celan, Piotr Rawicz, Primo Levi and many others took their own lives? Is that why a painter and Holocaust survivor I got to know refused medical treatment and died prematurely? Perhaps it was because he had given his testimony, said everything there was to be said. Perhaps it was because he could not give his testimony and, therefore, could not live any longer.

The difference between living to tell the tale and telling the tale to live is significant. The latter suggests that survival is the primary aim of us all, particularly of those who were spared the gas chambers. Fackenheim's famous formulation, his 614th commandment that originated at the symposium referred to above, speaks to the difference: "The authentic Jew of today is forbidden to hand Hitler yet another, posthumous victory."[5] He or she must survive as a Jew. The survivors who testified to their ordeal made it possible for themselves to stay alive. We, who were not there, are duty-bound to encourage them to tell and tell again to spare them from annihilation and save ourselves from dangerous ignorance.

Elie Wiesel may have described the reason for his own writing as a way of justifying his survival, rather than a means of survival, but his actions point in a different direction. He may have written *The Jews of Silence* about Jews in the former Soviet Union, but the content is about Jews as survivors.[6] What he had to tell about them, in fact, contributed to their survival. Silence may be inevitable at times, but survival is the purpose always.

The transformation of silence into the struggle for survival is a long process. In its final stages it reflects what Robert Jay Lifton has described as "the survivor's *struggle for meaning,* for a sense of inner form."[7] But survival is also a break with silence, a transformation into a new paradigm. Just as the silence of Aaron was soon followed by his assertiveness (Leviticus 10:16–20), the silence of individual survivors was transformed into the collective assertiveness of the Jewish people. It became, in Lifton's language, "the survivor mission."[8] Whereas individuals could either keep silent and give Hitler posthumous victories, or speak and lie, the Jewish people acted to survive: hence Israel. But such action also challenged the events that led to the silence in an effort to ensure that the tragedy would not happen again. The State of Israel is not a consolation but a transformation. The Holocaust was the final and most cruel manifestation of a Jewish world ruled by anti-Semitism; silence was the natural response to that. Israel is the beginning of a new era, characterized by the rebirth of Jewish assertiveness in which survival is the primary aim; the response now is determined action. That is why the existence of Israel is so central to Holocaust theologians as diverse in their interpretations as Eliezer Berkovits, Emil Fackenheim and Richard Rubenstein.

Assertive action can easily deteriorate into triumphalism and fanaticism. When that happens, the Holocaust becomes an emotive tool in the rhetoric. The silence of the victims and survivors is being debased by the deafening noise of propagandists and demagogues. That is why we have to ask the obvious question: Survival for what? The first, and perhaps second, generation after the *Shoah* will be satisfied with Fackenheim's rationale: not to give Hitler a posthumous victory. But what about future generations? Will this negative answer be sufficient, or will they seek positive reasons for Jewish survival? When, not if, they do, we must tell them what all the generations of Jews that came before them were told: Care for the stranger, for you were strangers in the land of Egypt. Survival, even in suffering, leads to solidarity with all who suffer to ease the pain and thus help to "mend the world" so that suffering will be no more.

It is not a coincidence that Emil Fackenheim is now a resident of Israel and the author of a seminal book, *To Mend the World*.[9] Already in the 1967 symposium, Fackenheim insisted not only that "we are, first, commanded to survive as Jews, lest the Jewish people perish," but also that "we are forbidden, finally, to despair of the world as the place which is to become the kingdom of God, lest we help make it a meaningless place in which God is dead or irrelevant and everything is permitted."[10] And Wiesel, having testified to the need for silence and the imperative of survival, turned in solidarity to the oppressed of other nations. As a survivor, he not only had a duty, but also a right to speak and act to prevent a universal holocaust and ease the personal suffering anywhere in the world.

Reflecting on this discussion of Wiesel's work, and paraphrasing his message, Robert McAfee Brown writes:

> The particularity of Jewish suffering can never be remembered only as an end in itself; it is a foretaste of what can happen to any person, any people. If Jews can be burned, so can others. To start with a concern for his own people — as Wiesel always does — is never to end there; it becomes, in turn, a starting place for concern for all peoples. The most Jewish of writers becomes the most universal among them.[11]

In this, Wiesel reverses the logic of prophecy. Whereas the prophets address Israel out of the actions of the nations, "the most Jewish of writers" of our time speaks to the nations out of the experience of Israel. He had broken his silence not only to survive by honouring the dead, but to prevent the death of others.

In a thoughtful paper, Fred L. Downing points to a development in the writings of Wiesel. Recalling his early years in Sighet, Wiesel writes as the *homo religiosus*. To find meaning in survival, he becomes a *homo poeta,* "man, the meaning maker," in which he reveals "a heroic effort to deny death ultimate victory" and pointing to "a courageous and prolific human project to reconstruct and restructure meaning on the ruins of a former life-world." This, finally, manifests itself in Wiesel, the *homo publicus* when this "private and sensitive man is driven into the realm of public advocacy for the purpose of the public enactment of a vision and the building of a more just and humane society."[12]

Although Downing does not put it this way, it may be legitimate to identify the *homo religiosus* as the Jew of silence in the face of God's unfathomable will, an Aaron-like figure; the *homo poeta* as the writer-survivor in search of meaning; and the *homo publicus* as the eminent Jew of our time who expresses the solidarity of his people with all who suffer out of his own and his people's indescribable pain.

The final chapter of Marc Ellis's book *Toward a Jewish Theology of Liberation* is called "From Holocaust to Solidarity." Recognizing the shift from silence to survival in Jewish life, Ellis speaks of "the need for empowerment as a religious response to destruction."[13] He believes that Jewish thought today must not centre around anti-Semitism because "the slogan 'Never Again' too often becomes the rationale for refusing to trust and to risk," whereas solidarity demands precisely such trust and risk.[14] We must tell the tale not only to honour our martyrs of the past, but to prevent martyrdom, in the present and in the future. "The new urgency, represented by the 'burning children' of all peoples, calls us to this rediscovery with a bewildering urgency: As much as any time in history, the world needs this witness, and at the crossroads of our own history, so do we."[15]

Robert McAfee Brown speaks the same language when he compares Wiesel's *The Town Beyond the Wall* to a short story by Albert Camus in which "the conclusion leaves unresolved whether a word written in tiny letters on the center of an artist's canvas should be read as solitary or solidary." Brown adds: "The shape of one letter was the infinite distance between isolation and community, between darkness and light."[16] The shift from solitary silence via survival, in search of meaning towards participatory solidarity suggests a conclusion that makes living possible for the survivor, even after he or she has told the tale. And it makes living possible for all of us because the one who has been through hell has addressed us. Those who have followed Wiesel's example have made the same journey from darkness to light. Paradoxically, by becoming conscious of the prospect of a global holocaust, life has gained more depth — despite the awareness of the danger or perhaps because of it.

McAfee Brown sees in this transformation of silence to solidarity a truly religious pilgrimage: "We have seen that the cumulative journey of the first five books [by Wiesel] was from solitude to solidarity, from looking into the visible face of death to looking into the invisible face of God."[17] God alone has the truly universal perspective; human beings can only speak out of their own narrow world and limited experience. But by seeking to reach out to the world at large through our particularity, we begin to perceive "the invisible face of God." Showing solidarity thus becomes the stuff out of which the theology of liberation is made — not only the liberation of others, but the liberation of self. It is in this universalist dimension that the survivor finds purpose, meaning and challenge. The survivor now knows the answer to the question: Survival for what? and can teach us its significance.

The silence of Aaron in the face of tragedy was soon transformed to assertiveness; he had to speak to survive. In time, he became the role model for all: "Be of the disciples of Aaron, one that loves peace, that loves mankind and brings them to Torah." (Avot 1:12) The formulation is deliberately universalist. The man or woman who has suffered and survived can care for humanity. We are urged to follow in his or her footsteps.

Does it matter? Can the powerless speak? Can survivors be heard or are they invariably ignored? Why speak at all? Indeed, why survive? Answer: to testify; in Walter Brueggemann's terminology, to make history. For Brueggemann, the Bible is not about recording history but about making history, because "the history-making process in ancient Israel is done through the voice of marginality which was carried by prophetic figures and those with whom they make common cause."[18] The most prominent among them is Jeremiah.

"My thesis, thus, is," writes Brueggemann, "that Jeremiah, as a voice of marginality, is a history-maker in the sense that the kings could not be, though he stands outside the time-line and outside every headline."[19]

Wiesel the survivor identifies with Jeremiah. At the end of his portrait of the prophet, he tells how Jeremiah defied the king. Then he adds, "And what are we doing, we writers, we witnesses, we Jews? For over 3,000 years, we have been repeating the same story — the story of a solitary prophet who would have given anything, including his life, to be able to tell another kind of tale, one filled with joy and fervor, rather than sorrow and anguish."[20] But he could not because he was called to higher things. "The history makers," writes Brueggemann, "are those who have the capacity and courage to *disclose* the human process. The dominant voices, however, are those which want to *close* the human process in the interest of order and the protection of a monopoly which always needs to be guarded." He adds, "Where history making ends, society is at the edge of losing its humaneness."[21]

Wiesel broke his silence to survive, but — by his own admission — he writes and speaks to testify. Much of that testimony, with the testimonies of other survivors, has made history precisely because it stood up to the dominant voices that clamour for the status quo, for the atrocities to continue — against Jews and non-Jews alike. The call to solidarity overpowers them, however; the voice of God is the voice of liberation, and Wiesel is one of its carriers. His message, articulating the message of the Jewish people, which includes suffering but transcends it, contains the voice of God that in its ostensible marginality makes history.

The attempt to make solidarity, not survival, the ultimate reason for breaking the silence in the face of the Holocaust, is also a deliberate effort to counteract those political forces that, within Jewry, see the *Shoah* as the moral validator of actions calculated to separate Jew from gentile, and those manifestations of power that, outside the Jewish community, view the Holocaust as the barrier between Jew and non-Jew. The Jews who insist that the Holocaust be invoked to validate everything we do, right or wrong, and the non-Jews — Christians, Muslims and secularists — who insist that we must cease to speak of it to gain recognition, are Holocaust abusers. The former because they separate solidarity from survival; the latter because they separate survival from solidarity. Both nationalist extremists, with their slogan "Never Again!", and international revisionists, who insist that it never happened, abuse the Holocaust.

Each time we refer to the quest for survival in relation to the existence of Israel, we are in danger of linking the two in a logical sequence in which the Holocaust justifies Israel. This is, of course, historically untrue, though it may be at times politically expedient. Wiesel makes the point repeatedly: the Holocaust is not a reason for Israel; Israel is at best a consolation for the Holocaust and an opportunity to care for the world precisely because Jews can call a fragment of that world their own.

Similarly, it may not be prudent to quote Wiesel's statement that even survivors did not always believe what happened to them. For it can be taken in evidence by Holocaust deniers. Yet I included the reference as an illustration of the magnitude of the experience and to remind ourselves that disbelief and denial come easily to us in the face of suffering and danger. Both lead to silence. Therefore, we must help each other remain alert in our common endeavours to prevent a future global holocaust. We must speak to live and to let live. Survival leads to solidarity, and solidarity leads to survival. Silence must be overcome, despite the pain of speaking. Wiesel has shown us how to do it.

Notes

1 George Steiner, note on republishing "The Hollow Miracle" in his *Language and Silence* (Harmondsworth: Penguin, 1969), 136.

2 Emil Fackenheim et al., "Jewish Values in the Post-Holocaust Future," *Judaism* 16:3 (Summer 1967): 285.

3 Ibid., 284.

4 Ibid.

5 Ibid, 272.

6 Elie Wiesel, *The Jews of Silence* (New York: Holt, Rinehart and Winston, 1966).

7 Robert Jay Lifton, "The Concept of the Survivor," in *The Future of Immortality* (New York: Basic Books, 1987), 241. Italics in original.

8 Ibid.

9 Emil Fackenheim, *To Mend the World* (New York: Schocken, 1982).

10 Fackenheim, "Jewish Values," 273.

11 Robert McAfee Brown, *Elie Wiesel — Messenger to all Humanity* (Notre Dame: University of Notre Dame Press, 1983), 16.

12 Fred L. Dowing, "Autobiography, Fiction, and Faith: Reflections on the Literary Religious Pilgrimage of Elie Wiesel" (paper presented at "Remembering for the Future," the International Scholars' Conference, Oxford, July 1988), 1441–55.

13 Marc H. Ellis, *Toward a Jewish Theology of Liberation* (Maryknoll, N.Y.: Orbis Books, 1987), 111.

14 Ibid., 114.

15 Ibid., 122.

16 McAfee Brown, 80.

17 Ibid., 99.

18 Walter Brueggemann, *Hope Within History* (Atlanta: John Knox Press, 1987), 55.

19 Ibid., 56. Italics in original.

20 Elie Wiesel, *Five Biblical Portraits* (Notre Dame: University of Notre Dame Press, 1981), 126–7.

21 Brueggemann, 57. Italics in original.

16

Social Action and Reform Judaism

One of the fundamental changes that is taking place in Jewish life is that Jewish law, *halachah*, has become inoperative for most Jews. Thus, according to their own self-definition, only 10 percent of American Jews describe themselves as Orthodox. And it is only Orthodox Jews who still claim that Jewish law is operative in their lives. The figures in Israel are not much higher for Orthodox allegiance and, of course, the State of Israel is not run according to Jewish law.

Halachah has power over few Jews nowadays. Many more — for example Conservative Jews in the United States and Reform Jews in Britain — pay lip service to it. They use it selectively and whimsically in a way Canadian sociologist of religion Reginald Bibby has described as religion à la carte.[1]

Had *halachah* been operative today, the terms of reference for social action in contemporary Judaism would have been clear. For Jewish law governs all aspects of Jewish life, not only that which is often described as *beyn adam lamakom,* 'between humanity and God,' but also *beyn adam lechavero,* 'between one human being and another.' There are, therefore, definite laws in traditional Judaism about how we should treat each other, individually and

Reprinted from *Manna* 21 (Autumn 1988): 21–3.

collectively. But once that law ceased to be binding, we lost the basis and have been left with no clear formula for action.

Yet we still have the need. Judaism can never be abstract theory. It must always be practical action. Therefore, though *halachah* may no longer be an acceptable norm for most Jews, *mitzvah* is. *Mitzvah*, 'commandment,' implies an action commanded by God. And God is affirmed by many more Jews than is Jewish law. Though only 10 percent of all Jews describe themselves as Orthodox, many more believe in God. Hence the need to do something to express this faith, even if Jews are irritated by the demands of the legalistic framework of Judaism. They want not only to be Jews but also to do Jewish things, although they are not prepared to view such actions as legally binding. Even Orthodox thinker Rabbi Irving Greenberg alludes to this when he speaks of "voluntary covenant" after the *Shoah*.[2]

The distinction between *halachah* and *mitzvah* is important for another reason: it enables non-Orthodox Jews to affirm revelation without falling into the trap of legalism. By seeking to express God's commandment, *mitzvah*, we can be true to our tradition and yet free of the constraints of a system of law, *halachah*, and thus have a basis for non-Orthodox observance.

For a long time, Jews found it difficult to do "Jewish things" in the realm of *beyn adam lamakom*, 'between humanity and God,' because that implied ritual. In fact, a major reason Reform Judaism developed was in answer to the need of many Jews to shed those rituals that separated them from the rest of the population. Such rituals were often described as "ceremonial" and not infrequently linked with hypocrisy and mindlessness. By contrast, actions to be performed *beyn adam lechavero*, 'between people,' were deemed authentic, primary and sincere: they were ethical.

There arose thus a sharpened division between the ritual/ceremonial and ethics, often expressed as social action. And ethics was considered superior to ritual. Did not the Hebrew prophets, the supreme exponents of ethics, castigate the priests, the practitioners of ritual? Did not, in later times, the Pharisees, the heirs of the biblical prophetic tradition, stand against the Sadducees, the conservative exponents of the priestly party? Should not we Reform Jews emulate the prophets and the Pharisees?

There was, of course, a more tangible reason why Reform Jews wanted to concentrate on ethics and ignore ritual. In the same way as ritual separated Jews from gentiles, ethics would bind Jew to gentile. Whereas emphasis on ritual belonged to the world of the ghetto, where Jews lived apart, the stress on ethics belonged to the age of emancipation, when Jews sought integration in society. And Reform Judaism was the expression of integrationist, emancipated Judaism. By minimizing ritual and maximizing ethics, Reform could present Judaism as a worthy partner in influencing, perhaps even shaping, the new society. Reform congregations were proud when their rabbi appeared beside the archbishop and the cardinal on behalf of homeless mothers or against the exploitation of children, advocating food for the hungry or opposing oppression in some far-away land. This stressed ethics and integration. Social action became the tangible expression of Reform Judaism, particularly in North America.

It also came to distinguish Reform from Orthodox and, to a large extent, Conservative Judaism. Internally, the differences were noticeable in how Reform Jews prayed or ate or celebrated, but the outside world was only dimly aware of those differences. Externally the differences were reflected in the Reform involvement in social action and the absence of others in this work. Although *halachah* provides for social action, and Orthodox Jews as adherents of *halachah* are commanded to practise it, another element entered into Orthodoxy. It was always there but it was more prominent when juxtaposed with the spirit of emancipation: the making of boundaries. In contrast to Reform, Orthodoxy feared the outside world and wished to separate itself from it, because it stressed the danger of assimilation. Therefore, it kept away from undue involvement with the non-Jewish world. Ethical conduct and social action were stressed as long as they were carried out from Jew to Jew — not from Jew to gentile. That is why Orthodox communities remain strong in their support for one another, but largely indifferent to the outside world.

In many ways, modern anti-Semitism has vindicated this approach and many Jews, who would describe themselves as secular, have taken it up. They see themselves as ethical persons with a deep social conscience, but they are not prepared to waste it on potentially hostile gentiles. Working in the Jewish community and for Israel are the primary manifestations of *mitzvah* among the secularists.

Many of them are likely to be members of Reform congregations for a host of irrelevant reasons. Civil religion is a primary force in contemporary Jewish life. With many other Jews, members of Reform congregations have become not only economically affluent, but philosophically bourgeois and middle-class in every sense. We know the middle classes love philanthropy, which they identify as ethical conduct, but are suspicious of social action because it smacks of leftist politics. They also suspect social action because it is collectivist, whereas individualism is central to the way of life of most of our members. They want their help to go to specifically designated individuals and groups, not anonymously to the common good. Hence the need for plaques, people honoured at events and all the other artificial structures that pander to bourgeois individualism and dominate Jewish life in the United States and elsewhere.

Now we can understand why the impulse to social action, once so prominent in Reform Judaism, has weakened in recent decades. We have many secular Jews in our midst, and we are mostly middle-class. The former makes for isolationism and the latter for disdain for the masses. The combination puts brakes on social action and intensifies our work for Israel, which simultaneously meets the needs for philanthropy and isolationism. That is why we must try harder. Instead of being overwhelmed by isolationism in our midst, we must seek to counteract it. To do so, we not only need enthusiasm and tenacity, but a theoretical basis, a theology of social action.

As it cannot be Jewish law, what could it be? What are the theoretical foundations of social action in contemporary Reform Judaism? Let me offer only two arguments. The one I shall call historic and the other mystical, for I believe both are competing to fill the vacuum created by the end of legalism in Jewish life.

The historic reason for social action is best expressed in the many statements in Scripture about how to behave well to the downtrodden, whoever and wherever they may be — because we were slaves in Egypt. Whereas psychology may suggest that the downtrodden oppress others when they get a chance to do so, our theology insists that, because we have suffered, we must ease the suffering of others when we are given the means. Such action cannot be a matter of discretion. It is a question of duty. It is not charity but justice. Jewish power, to be authentic, must be exercised with the memory of powerlessness, because our memory as Jews is the key to our morality as Jews.

This, then, is the first reason why we must be in the forefront of social action: we have been on the other side, so we know what it is like. Now that we have "arrived," we are duty-bound to help others. In this scheme of things, as members of the middle class we have assumed additional responsibilities to be open to the world, not to have found more reasons for shutting it out.

The second reason for social action in this post-halachic age is mystical. In the Jewish mystical tradition much is made of the idea that the world is incomplete and our task as human beings is to complete it. This complex and difficult notion is often described as *tikkun olam,* 'mending the world.' Whatever it may mean theologically and philosophically, it offers a helpful metaphor for social action. We are doing things, performing *mitzvot,* as a way of helping to make the world a better place, of mending it. We have been created by God for this task. God has revealed the divine will to humanity through the people of Israel to tell us how to do it. When we are doing what our Creator revealed to us, we are working towards the redemption of the world.

Creation, revelation and redemption are the three categories of Jewish theology. Social action is their practical manifestation and thus our contribution to the redemption of the as-yet-unredeemed, but divinely created, world. As in mysticism, each *mitzvah* has a practical and psychological value and assumes cosmic significance. And although it is not for any of us to eradicate all evil in the world, each of us, as the late Abraham Joshua Heschel has urged us, can remove some evils. And if enough of us help to remove evils, evil will disappear and the world will be mended.

Here the historical and the mystical dimensions converge, since the purpose of history is also redemption — freedom for our people — which is only possible when freedom has been achieved by all peoples. The promise given to our ancestors can, ultimately, only be fulfilled when the world has been perfected. The two reasons for social action are not alternatives but complementary.

Even this brief and inadequate excursion into mysticism offers a spiritually compelling reason for social action, although the historical argument may be more easily accessible and less complicated and abstract. It removes, of course, all considerations of expediency and, almost by definition, does not require any external reward. *S'char mitzvah — mitzvah*, our sages taught, the reward of a *mitzvah* is doing the *mitzvah*. It can be performed whether you believe it to be legally binding or "merely" morally compelling; whether you are a mystic or just someone who wants to be helpful. Once you accept its presupposition, all other reasons become unnecessary. It is also irrelevant to ask questions about who the recipient is — Jew or gentile, someone congenial or not — because the act makes the world a better place, even if it does not make the doer feel better. It is not even relevant to ask if your single action is going to solve the problem. If it alleviates it, however slightly, you are justified in doing it, because helping to bring the world towards redemption is always of value. It is, ultimately, a qualitative and not a quantitative act.

Both the reasons given here, the historic and the mystical, base social action in Jewish tradition and in the religious life. Now, it is possible that some, or many, Reform Jews who are engaged in this work do it almost as a substitute for Judaism and for spirituality. The Jewish answer to this would be: so what? Our religious heritage is very cautious in judging motives. It is much more interested in results.

When Abraham Isaac Kook, the first Chief Rabbi of Israel, saw the pioneers in the land of Israel of the 1920s and 1930s drain the swamps and turn the desert into arable land while proclaiming themselves to be atheists and disregarding every manifestation of observance, he did not castigate them, although he was pained by the negation of a recognizable Jewish lifestyle. He saw that they were redeeming the land and thus doing God's work in spite of themselves. If he could accept them then, we can now accept our social activists, whatever their motives. As the pioneers then were vindicated by their results, so let us hope that our pioneers now will be vindicated by theirs.

Notes

1 Reginald W. Bibby, *Fragmented Gods* (Toronto: Irwin Publishing, 1987), especially chapter 4.

2 Irving Greenberg, *Voluntary Covenant* (New York: Jewish National Resource Center, 1982).

17

Should the Canadian Jewish Community Be Involved in Social Issues?

Jews have gained access to power. Emil Fackenheim, the philosopher, describes the contemporary Jewish condition as our people's re-entry into history.[1] Yehuda Bauer, the historian, speaks of the modern Jew's emergence from powerlessness. Rabbi Irving Greenberg, the vociferous campaigner for Jewish unity, analyzes the present situation as the dawn of a third major epoch in Jewish history.[2] That Jews have power is, of course, particularly true in Israel. But it is also true in those Diaspora countries that have large Jewish populations; the United States is the most obvious example, but Canada should also be included.

During my sojourn in Canada, I have perceived that Canadian Jewry is not a powerless minority, but a significant component of the national mosaic. Most Jews in Canada belong to the privileged strata of the population, financially, politically, intellectually, educationally. This also seems to be taken for granted — more with genuine admiration and respect than with malice and envy — by many non-Jews.

It is something that many Jews tend to deny; in fact, some activities of the organized Jewish community are born out of that

Reprinted from *Viewpoints* 14:4 (1986).

denial and may account for the surprise they often create among the Canadian public. If other Canadians do not perceive us as underprivileged, but we see ourselves as vulnerable, our actions become incongruous. What most Canadians cannot know, of course, is that you can take the Jew out of the ghetto, but you cannot take the ghetto mentality out of the Jew.

The Jewish self-perception is understandable, for we are recent arrivals from the ghetto. We may have adapted with remarkable ease to the outer trappings of the open society, but we have not yet integrated these with our real feelings. Socially, we behave as if we were at home in Canada but, emotionally, we react as if we still lived in Russia, Poland, Romania or Hungary.

This is a major factor in our reluctance to be involved, as a community, in the social issues of Canadian society. Yes, we will encourage individual Jews to play a part in humanitarian efforts and even be proud of their achievements. But collectively, we tend to stick to specifically Jewish issues. As a result, we appear more committed to self-defence than to the betterment of society. When we engage as a community in projects aimed at improving the quality of life in Canada, it is often as a by-product of our self-interest or a belief that it is useful for our public-relations image. All this suggests that we often apply a ghetto attitude to our non-ghetto existence and end up confusing ourselves and others.

I am the last person to suggest that we should deny or forget our ghetto existence; or that we should adopt a naive faith in the goodness of all humanity. On the contrary. My aim is to reiterate and apply Greenberg's formula: "Exercise of power must be accompanied by strong models and constant evocation of the memory of historic Jewish suffering and powerlessness. It is so easy to forget slavery's lessons once one is given power, but such forgetfulness leads to the unfeeling infliction of power over others . . . Memory is the key to morality."[3]

The Exodus from Egypt is what Fackenheim has called a root-experience; it not only shaped our history but decided our actions since.[4] The call to love the stranger, because we were strangers in the land of Egypt, is repeated frequently in the Torah. As we have gained access to power, it must be understood as a commandment to apply the experience of slavery by fighting for the freedom of all the oppressed. Whereas once we could only plead for ourselves, now we must use our resources where before we could only use our words — to champion the cause of others. Psychological theory may suggest that those once oppressed tend to identify themselves with oppressors when the opportunity arises. But theological reality, as taught by our tradition, insists on the opposite. Because we know the bitterness of oppression, we owe it to God to manifest our solidarity with all oppressed and fight for their redemption.

If we are serious about our Judaism, and if we really want to enhance its fundamental teachings, not only its quaint rituals, we should find a formula for our own action. If the story of the Exodus matters to us, not only at pleasant family gatherings around the *seder* table, we must take the consequences and emulate the prophets. We must do so, even if it provokes the ire of others who want to enjoy the fruits of their power without discharging their responsibilities.

This kind of understanding of Judaism not only bridges some gaps between religious denominations but also enables so-called secular Jews to express themselves Jewishly without committing themselves religiously. You don't have to be religious to have a biblical/theological perspective on the place of social action in Judaism.

To make my case, let me refer to Greenberg, an Orthodox rabbi, who suggests that the shift from powerlessness to power has also led to greater secularity. He speaks, in fact, of "holy secularity" replacing theology after the Holocaust, when it has become so difficult to be explicit about God. It is an understanding of Judaism that points directly to the principles of social action:

> We are entering a period of silence in theology — a silence that corresponds to profound hiddenness. The fundamental religious act is the reaffirmation of faith, redemption and meaningfulness through acts of love and giving . . . In an age when one is ashamed or embarrassed to talk about God in the presence of burning children, the creation of an image of God — *viz.,* a

> human being of infinite value, equality and uniqueness
> — is an act that speaks even louder than words.[5]

Social action can become the unifying force in the Jewish world today. Those who hold different theological views, and those who reject theology altogether, can join forces in acts of love and giving affirming the human being of infinite value, equality and uniqueness. Even if we are not in a position to explain or eradicate evil, we probably can remove some evils and thus help to "mend the world."

These reflections warrant the aside that the affirmation of social-action programmes, arising out of an "ecumenical" understanding of the contemporary Jewish condition, would be enormously helpful in persuading alienated Jews that the Jewish community has something to offer them and that it needs their talents. Many Jews look upon the community with disdain, because they see it as parochial and ghettoized, pre-occupied with self-seeking and obsessed with squabbles between various interest groups. And they want no part of that.

Perhaps the leaders of Canadian Jewry, who so audibly lament the alienation of some of our best people, would improve things by resolute action. This would show that we are concerned for society and can unite to further its welfare, not only in the face of anti-Semitism and in response to the danger to the State of Israel, but also on intrinsic merits. An intensified social-action programme would have wide and beneficial ramifications, besides being a real test of our emancipation. It is part of the programme for Jewish continuity.

The call to social action does not go against our commitment to our own community and the State of Israel. On the contrary, fighting evils does not preclude the evils that befall our own people, and championing the cause of justice always includes justice for Jews. To make a strong case, we must begin with ourselves and aim at making the Jewish community a model and an example, not a martyr. As Greenberg puts it, "after Auschwitz, martyrdom is morally offensive. The command is to live and to testify . . . how to use the power is the new *halacha,* but denial or endangering the power is considered the unforgivable sin."[6]

Jews who, in the name of some unidentified universalism, neglect their own in favour of global issues, usually deploy assimilationist subterfuges. Despite their lofty principles and considerable achievements, there is little reason for the Jewish community to take pride in them. Any Jew who diminishes the strength of his people commits an unforgivable sin. If he, or she, doesn't know it, it is our duty to remind him or her.

We start with ourselves, by caring for our community, for we are duty-bound to make sure Israel comes first. To endanger our own is as morally offensive as to threaten someone else's. That has always been true; it is especially so after Auschwitz.

But we don't stop with ourselves. The fact that we have left the ghetto does not absolve us from responsibility to fellow Jews, but it extends our obligations far beyond our own circles. As Martin Buber put it: "To begin with oneself, but not to end with oneself; to start from oneself, but not to aim at oneself; to comprehend oneself, but not to be preoccupied with oneself."[7]

In trying to answer "Should the Canadian Jewish community be involved in social issues?" I have assumed that the reference is to activities that go beyond the needs of the Jewish community and the State of Israel. My answer to the question is: Yes, the Canadian Jewish community should be involved in social issues. My theological basis for this conclusion is simple. Our religious heritage is deliberately partisan in favour of the disadvantaged. Therefore, we are obligated to live up to the teachings of Judaism by reaching out to all who are in need. Since we are now full partners in Canadian society, we are duty-bound to manifest this, reaching beyond the confines of the Jewish community, but never at its expense. The following are some examples of how we can do it.

The first area that comes to mind, following the principle that charity begins at home, has to do with economic justice in Canada. Many of us have "made it" in the open society; many Jews and non-Jews have not. With time, the economic imbalance has increased, exacerbated in recent years by massive unemployment, an apparently inescapable by-product of our economic system. As Jews, we have a tradition of the dignity of labour and the importance for each person to be able to earn his, or her, livelihood. It is, therefore, incumbent upon us to engage in activities that promote economic justice, whether or not they serve our personal, financial and political interests. Special attention should be paid to the physically and mentally disabled, refugees and similar groups that cannot fend for themselves. To exercise power with the memory of powerlessness means precisely that.

It also means that we must ally ourselves with those forces that champion the cause of women and demand equal pay for work of equal value. Even Orthodox Jews who believe that, in matters of worship and observance, men and women have separate responsibilities, will still insist on the intrinsic equality of the sexes.

Many religious leaders in Canada, notably members of the United Church and the Catholic Bishops, have made wide-ranging, courageous recommendations in matters of economic justice, unemployment, organized labour, women's rights and related subjects. Even if the Jewish community does not have the resources to act on its own, it should lend its support and endorse many of these recommendations. This would also give substance to Jewish-Christian co-operation, taking it beyond its present, still relatively narrow, confines of civility and platitudes. By working together for new structures, not merely engaging in Victorian philanthropy, we would put our common sense of purpose to the test.

Other activities exist where co-operation with secular, rather than religious, groups may prove more fruitful. Thus, out of our concern for the dignity of life and as Jews, we have something to say about such controversial topics as abortion, euthanasia and capital punishment.

Unlike some religious groups, Jews give priority to the life of the mother over her unborn child. This does not mean that Judaism condones abortion on demand, but it has a less-than-rigid attitude to abortion. It should be advocated as a way of preserving traditional values, while respecting the integrity of individuals.

Similarly, because Jews believe that life is infinite and not quantifiable, no human being should be allowed to end it at will. This does not, however, obligate us to prolong it unduly by artificial means. The medical profession would welcome our guidance on this issue.

Capital punishment, as a third example, is abhorrent for Jews and could only be justified in the face of indisputable evidence that it saves innocent lives. Without such evidence, we must oppose it. Let no Jew be lured into supporting capital punishment by quoting Scripture. He or she must also take history and current practice into account, including the fact that capital punishment does not exist in the State of Israel, even for terrorists.

I am painfully aware that I have listed, in almost cavalier fashion, a range of issues each of which requires detailed analysis and debate. I also know that objections could be raised pointing to the risk of getting involved. Let us bear in mind, however, that the risk of no action is greater than the risk of mistaken action.

When we lived in the ghetto, we often decided moral issues by asking: *Gut oder schlecht far di Yidn?*, 'Is it good or bad for the Jews?' When we lived in isolation and without power, we had no choice but to leave the affairs of society to others. As emancipated Jews we cannot do so. The question whether it is good or bad for the Jews is still valid. The answer, however, now implies that what is good for society and for the world is good for the Jews, even when it does not always seem so at first glance. It is time we learned that lesson — and acted on it.

Notes

1 Emil L. Fackenheim, *The Jewish Return into History* (New York: Schocken, 1978).

2 Irving Greenberg, *The Third Great Cycle in Jewish History* (New York: National Jewish Resource Center, 1981).

3 Ibid., 25.

4 Emil L. Fackenheim, *God's Presence in History* (New York: Harper Torchbooks, 1970), 8–14.

5 Greenberg, 16.

6 Ibid., 25.

7 Quoted in *Forms of Prayer for Jewish Worship: Daily and Sabbath* (London: The Reform Synagogues of Great Britain, 1977), 118.

Neighbours

The previous section of this volume sought to point out that Diaspora existence obligates Jews to be full partners in all concerns of society at large. The four chapters that now follow discuss our theoretical involvement with the non-Jewish world. The implication is that solidarity and dialogue are closely related.

The greatest impediment to dialogue between Jews and non-Jews is, of course, anti-Semitism. Though chapters 18 and 19 cover similar ground, they reflect different aspects of the problem. Neither holds out much hope for global mutual understanding, and the pessimistic tone is reinforced by Chapter 20.

As a counterbalance, Chapter 21 offers a much more positive perspective. Much of what I have written on the subject of Christian-Jewish relations, in this book and elsewhere, suggests that as difficult as it may be to find a firm basis for an open relationship between Christianity and Judaism, it is possible and desirable to establish good lines of communication between *Christians* and *Jews*.

In providing a moving example of how this can be done, this concluding chapter should also be read as an expression of hope that Jews and Christians will continue to engage in activities that foster such personal encounters and enrich the faith of each. In this too, Israel may be the catalyst.

18

Jews and Gentiles:
A Changing Relationship

Existentialist philosophers distinguish between authentic and inauthentic existence. Although authentic existence is hard to define, its opposite is more open to description. It is an existence determined by others so that, in the end, I see myself only as others perceive me. A measure of such inauthenticity may be inescapable in life. But when the criteria of others become the only, or principal, tools of self-understanding, the individual or group loses its identity.

Since the emancipation, Jews have often been victims of inauthentic existence, that is, they have viewed themselves with the eyes of the non-Jewish world. Although Jewish self-hatred is older than emancipation, it was during the post-emancipation period that it was particularly evident. In their efforts to be accepted into the non-Jewish world, many Jews looked at themselves and Judaism with non-Jewish eyes. They tried desperately to live up to the expressed expectations of the majority culture. One way to achieve their objectives was to agree with the hostile critique of Jews and Judaism and then show they were different.

That was probably one reason why German Jews, well on their way to acculturation, looked down on the *Ostjuden,* the Jews from eastern Europe whose language and dress so closely identified them as Jews. It was for the same reason that, in North America, the older

Reprinted from *Viewpoints* 17:2 (1989).

Jewish settlers looked down on the "greeners." Later, when religion ceased to be the dominant force in the surrounding culture and Jews no longer had to "Christianize" their Judaism but to "secularize" it, they founded other institutions that would emulate the non-Jewish world. The Jewish golf-and-country club is a typical example.

That these new Jewish institutions were deeply conscious of anti-Semitism adds to the irony; Jews wanted to be like the others, but the others would not let them. Therefore, they emulated the others within a new kind of ghetto by creating imitation institutions. Those whom they wished to emulate forced them to remain in their own Jewish corner. The yearning to assimilate was thwarted by the role models. God works in mysterious ways to preserve the people of Israel.

Anti-Semitism, which has flourished since the emancipation, is therefore a central pre-occupation of assimilationists. As hard as they try to be like the others, the others make sure the Jews remain different. Observant Jews of whatever denomination have enough positive reasons for being Jewish to contain the hatred, even the persecution, by non-Jews. The non-observant do not have such causes for affirmation, so every anti-Semitic utterance pains them out of proportion.

Anti-Semitism bestows upon the assimilated Jews much of their Jewish identity. They will tell a rabbi with pride that they are not observant and not religious but "proud to be a Jew." And how does this pride manifest itself? When someone made an anti-Semitic remark they punched him on the nose, or left the premises, or did something equally "heroic." No amount of rabbinic eloquence will persuade this "proud" Jew that it is a pity our enemies, rather than our tradition and God, must define our identity.

Anti-Semitism is often explained away by eager assimilationists as isolated incidents resulting from poor education or unfortunate Jewish behaviour. If only "we" could present our Judaism, everybody would love us, or at least respect us. Better community relations is, therefore, the solution.

Much of the traditional post-emancipation relationship between Jews and gentiles was based on this premise. Hence the enthusiasm for the Anti-Defamation League, the Council of Christians and Jews, community relations committees and many similar organizations. There are many members of the congregation I serve who would not pay attention even to my Kol Nidre sermon but who will write me warm letters of deep affection on the strength of an unsolicited testimonial from a WASP across the road who had heard me preach in his or her church. If the gentile liked what I had to say, I must be good.

That is why Israel was such a source of *naches* for the assimilated. It showed the world that Jews could behave like gentiles, only more so. The Six Day War was a turning point in Jewish life. It enabled Jews to remain far away from Jewish living and yet take pride in being Jewish. The Israeli paratroopers expiated all the *Ostjuden* and "greeners." Inauthentic Judaism became vicarious Judaism. We could make progress towards integration in the gentile world thanks to the heroism of Jews whom we did not know and had no intention of joining.

The paradox of pride in Israel and refusal to live there deserves a moment of reflection. While Jews proclaim with gusto and enthusiasm the virtues of Jewish sovereignty, they are not prepared to do much for it. Even the money we send is not freely given, but extracted by peers whose success in canvassing decides their status as Jewish leaders. It is interesting, incidentally, that when Israel most needed the money, that is, in the very early years of its existence and before, Jews gave very little. Only after the Six Day War did the contributions from the Diaspora increase dramatically.

It is to this that we can also trace one cause of the failure of at–tempts to educate during fund-raising events. The organizers, especially if they are Israelis, think if they can increase Jewish knowledge, they will heighten commitment. They ignore the fact that, for many would-be participants, involvement with Israel is a substitute for commitment to Judaism and, therefore, they will react against study. They will attend lectures and gatherings for the same reasons that those who turn a deaf ear to my sermons in *shul* will laud my greatness because their non-Jewish neighbour heard me. When the study gets serious, rather than fashionable, most people drop out.

Let us also reflect on the Soviet Jewry campaign. Our vicarious Judaism compels us to urge others to go and live in Israel. The poor

Jews in the Soviet Union were considered highly suitable for this enterprise. But they too are largely assimilated. One reason many of them wanted to leave the then Soviet Union is because integration had been denied them. Israel was their means of liberation, but not their Promised Land. In Israel they would have to be Jews, whereas in the West they could assimilate more freely. That is why they prefer Toronto to Tel Aviv. It is also why, once they come to Toronto, they keep away from the community, and the community is not very keen on their presence either. After all, they are "greeners"; we are only prepared to accept those among them who are suitable for "yellowing."

But the situation may be changing. The assimilationist enterprise that tries to replace commitment to Judaism with the fight against anti-Semitism and support for Israel is failing. Israel is not a source of unmitigated pride, but a cause for considerable embarrassment. We cannot bask in the glory of Israel's defence forces, because controlling civilians is less glamorous than rescuing the hostages in Entebbe. Because we find out what we think by reading the papers, we are disturbed by the news items and the editorials about Israel. If you take the *New York Times* as your Torah, you are pained by the strictures of the queen of the American press. Hence the pre-occupation of the Jewish community with media misrepresentation of Israel. We are not making the desired good impression on the gentiles and that worries us enormously.

The only explanation we can think of is that it is all due to anti-Semitism. However, since none of the valiant efforts by the Canada-Israel Committee, and corresponding organization in other countries, seem to shift public opinion, we must revise our view about anti-Semitism. We do not see it as episodic, but as endemic, reflecting a permanent hostility to Jews; not against some other Jews, but against us! Like the assimilated Theodore Herzl at the Dreyfus trial, we see ourselves in the dock of the court of public opinion, and we are confused.

Once we recognize the confusion, we see anti-Semitism every-where. In fact, the surest way of attracting Jewish audiences today is to tell them that anti-Semitism is on the increase, and that we are all vulnerable. The ethos of Jewish communal life rests often on this premise. It is an ethos, however, that rarely returns us to our roots and the sources of Judaism. It has not prompted us to find those positive affirmations of Judaism, the absence of which made us so vulnerable to anti-Semitism in the first place. Instead, the new ethos imbues us with a misguided fighting spirit and a quixotic determination to remove all the obstacles to our total integration or assimilation. Our pre-occupation with anti-Semitism remains linked to our determination to be like everybody else. We must be defiant in the face of attacks. It does not occur to us to be more firmly rooted in our tradition. Thus Israeli actions must be defended not because we believe in them, but because the accusers must not be vindicated, even if they are right.

Why do I refuse to reckon with the possibility that Jewish despair over anti-Semitism is not self-seeking and neurotic, but motivated by the Jews' determination to build, here in Canada, a healthy society, free of prejudice? Because I fail to see much Jewish concern when other minorities are the victims of prejudice and persecution. I have not seen many Jewish expressions of solidarity with, for example, the blacks in Canada, who feel hounded and discriminated against by those entrusted with law enforcement, just as the Jews once were in the ghetto. There is, indeed, every reason to fight anti-Semitism, for it is an unmitigated evil. But our case is considerably weakened when we fight only anti-Semitism and turn a blind eye to the other injustices in our society.

We can do so with impunity because the society into which we seek integration is equally prejudiced against visible minorities. In fact, the more the majority culture picks on them, the more it leaves the Jews alone. Compared to blacks and Orientals, all Jews are white and acceptable.

A further change: the relationship between Jews and gentiles is not seen primarily in terms of Jews and Christians, as it once was. Ours has become a secularized society. That is why the Council of Christians and Jews is languishing and other similar activities have been marginalized. What brings Jews and Christians together today, albeit in rather low profile, is that they are in the same boat — both are in danger of being swamped by a culture that is indifferent to religion.

That is one reason why the religious institution has ceased to be the primary representative of the community; it has been replaced by ostensibly secular bodies. They are the new protagonists of civil religion.

I do not intend to extrapolate what will happen in the future from the present, but I would like to suggest what ought to happen.

All attempts to make our Judaism suit gentile prejudices have not only been pathetic, but futile. Jews trying to minimize or hide their Jewishness have not earned the respect of the non-Jewish world. But Jews who have affirmed their origins and their faith, have. The quest for Jewish authenticity is a prerequisite for good gentile-Jewish relations. I do not have in mind a strident or defiant affirmation of Judaism — for that is invariably a sign of insecurity — but a quiet expression of standards and values and convictions and practices.

This means, paradoxically, that if a Jew wants to be accepted as an equal member of the open society, he or she must sort out his or her Jewish commitment first. This is particularly true in Canada where the cultural mosaic encourages and rewards those who remain true to their tradition. Being a Jew in Canada is conducive to espousing the traditional Jewish principles of *torah,* 'holy study,' *avodah,* 'worship' and *gemilut chassadim,* 'acts of loving kindness.' To be a knowledgeable Jew and a practising Jew makes it easier to be an integrated Canadian.

However, to get this far, at least one other obstacle must be overcome: the lure of modernity. We may no longer have to imitate the WASPs in the hope of being accepted by society. But we still believe that being an equal means to be part of the culture that values recreation more than religion, and consumerism more than contemplation. To recognize the futility of such vulgar modernity is a necessary challenge for every sensitive woman and man in our society. Jews are not exempt from the challenge; unless they are willing to be critical of modernity, they will find it very difficult to affirm their tradition. Being critical does not mean having to reject it, just not capitulating to it. Jewish authenticity demands from us creative social maladjustment.

Part of our critical apparatus must be directed towards the question of anti-Semitism. We must ask ourselves why we were once naive enough to believe that, if we only made a good impression on gentiles, anti-Semitism would go away. We must also ask ourselves why we have such a great need to exaggerate every anti-Semitic act. Of course, there is anti-Semitism in our society and, of course, we have to take steps to expose it and protect ourselves against it. But it is not the greatest threat to Jewish existence today. There are even cynics who would contend that it keeps us together, at least in the free world, more than it threatens us. Apathy, indifference to tradition and to matters of the spirit, is a much greater threat to our present and our future as Jews. By concentrating on anti-Semitism, we are evading the real issues and damaging ourselves under the guise of protecting ourselves. We would be much wiser to recognize anti-Semitism for what it is, namely a gentile disease, rather than to see its eradication as exclusively our problem.

To cure anti-Semitism, we must seek to cure the society that breeds it, and that means fighting every form of discrimination and championing every cause that promotes equality and social justice, that is, a healthy society. We would probably diminish anti-Semitism greatly if we devoted at least some of the energy we put into Jewish organizations dedicated to its eradication into causes that work for an overall better society. Solidarity with the disadvantaged will advance our cause more than will our present communal insularity. Our desire to be accepted by the society has — paradoxically again — driven us to an isolationism that defeats our purpose. We have built a ghetto to break down the ghetto. It is no wonder that our endeavours manifest themselves more in neuroses than in successes. We are fighting the wrong battles with the wrong weapons.

What has been said about our attitude to anti-Semitism can also be said about our defence of Israel. By stonewalling every expression of criticism of Israel and identifying every critic as an enemy of our people, we present ourselves as uncaring and unfeeling chauvinists. In our endeavours to be the defenders of Judaism by holding Israel as being beyond reproach, we express views that negate fundamental Jewish values; we are negating the biblical prophets and siding with their enemies. As a result, we are losing credibility. We would have a much greater impact on our non-Jewish neighbours if we shared our dilemmas and agonies over Israel. They might better understand if we explained to them — positively, not negatively as a hedge against anti-Semitism — why the return to the land is crucial to our faith and people and why, to retain sovereignty and to allow for democracy, Jews may sometimes compromise righteousness; why the return to the land has made it necessary to emulate Aaron, the accommodating priest, and not only to seek to be like Moses, the uncompromising prophet. And that other faiths and other peoples must face the same dilemmas and experience the same pain; that being critical of Israeli policies is no more a sign of disloyalty by Jews than being critical of Canadian policies is treason. Such an approach would elicit much greater understanding and support. If we refuse to criticize the government of Israel as we criticize other governments, we present ourselves as stooges or as zombies; in either, case we would be selling ourselves hopelessly short.

A radical approach is, therefore, required both in the critique of what has been done so far and of what needs to be done in the future. Jews have never had it so good in the Diaspora, and this is largely due to the existence of Israel. The new situation offers us almost limitless opportunities, but it puts before us enormous challenges. We must not escape either by deploying irrelevant myths and outdated ideas.

19

Christians, Jews and Anti-Semitism Now

We return to the theme of Jacob and Esau. The rabbinic view that regards Jacob as the archetypal Jew and Esau as the prototype for every gentile is rooted in the biblical account of the two brothers. The account in Genesis of their reunion is pertinent to the theme of this chapter:

> Looking up, Jacob saw Esau coming, accompanied by four hundred men. He divided the children among Leah, Rachel and the two maids, putting the maids and their children first, Leah and her children next, and Rachel and Joseph last. He himself went on ahead and bowed low to the ground seven times until he was near his brother. Esau ran to greet him. He embraced him and, falling on his neck, *vayishakehu*, he kissed him; and they wept. (Genesis 33:1–4)

The Masoretic text has, besides the vowels and cantillation signs, dots over each letter of the word *vayishakehu*, 'he kissed him.'[1] Rashi, the medieval Jewish commentator, reflecting rabbinic tradition, wrote: "Some explain the dotting as meaning that he (Esau) did not kiss him (Jacob) with his whole heart. However, R. Simon bar

Reprinted from the *Toronto Journal of Theology* 6:2 (Fall 1990).

Yochai said: Surely, it is well known that Esau hated Jacob, but at that moment his pity was really aroused and he kissed him with his whole heart."[2] In other words, the sages agreed about Esau's hatred of Jacob but differed about whether, in the moment of reunion, Esau forgot himself and showed genuine love for his bother. If so, the literal accuracy of the text could be upheld; otherwise a reinterpretation along Rashi's first suggestion, as implied in those additional dots, would be required.

Another rabbinic authority suggests we should not read the text as *vayishakehu*, 'he kissed him,' but *vayishachehu*, 'he bit him.'[3] Esau, the paradigmatic gentile, could not possibly kiss Jacob, the paradigmatic Jew, although they were brothers. Therefore — with a very slight change of the Masoretic text — we should assume that Esau the gentile, in fact, bit Jacob the Jew. This may be poor exegesis, but it is a telling illustration of how some Jews view the relationship between Jew and gentile.

Despite all the changes since rabbinic times, little has changed when it comes to the perception of Jews. Many are unable to distinguish between the gentile whom Esau represents and the Christian of today. Many Jews, probably the majority, are uncomfortable with, and even suspicious of, Christian-Jewish co-operation. That is why so few show interest in it.

Christian-Jewish dialogue is of little concern to most exponents of contemporary Judaism and a stepchild of Jewish creativity in our time. But in the days of Franz Rosenzweig, Leo Baeck and other giants of twentieth-century Jewish thought, it was central. As a member of that small minority of Jews to whom the matter is of concern now, I would like to report that those engaged in interfaith dialogue today are considered at best marginal and eccentric; more often they are suspected of more sinister motives. For example, they are suspected of having a desire to win the recognition from gentiles that is denied them among Jews.

The reason for the suspicion and the lack of interest is the widespread belief among Jews that the roots of anti-Semitism are found in Christian teachings and that, despite the evolution of Christian theology, very little has been done by those in authority to denounce the past and to radically reformulate the teachings of

Christianity. In recent years, this Jewish perception has been reinforced by a rich and revealing literature, written by Christians, that corroborates and reinforces the view that Christianity has sown the seeds of anti-Semitism all the way to the Holocaust and beyond. Jews have also noted that the authors of such books and articles have remained on, or been relegated to, the periphery of their respective churches, so that their conclusions could remain unheeded by the mainstream.

However, I find it most unhelpful to engage in the all-too-common activity of Jewish accusations calculated to elicit a mixture of Christian resentment and breast-beating. The above is only intended as a reminder that the past, and the lack of change in the present, are the reasons most Jews give for avoiding Christian-Jewish dialogue. They find it undignified and futile to engage in an activity that may produce some civility, a few media opportunities and one or two symbolic acts, but that does not alter the conventional Christian image of the Church triumphant and the Synagogue blindfolded.

More significant is the fact that those Jews who engage in Jewish-Christian dialogue often harbour the same presuppositions as those who do not. Even activists in the field may suspect that Esau, now the Christian brother, is bent on biting Jacob the Jew. But they hope that with suitable tact and education they can avert that intention in favour of a real kiss. Many of those Jews who engage in dialogue — and they are a minority — do so in the quixotic hope of eliminating, or at least lessening, anti-Semitism. They believe that by making a good impression, the Jew can persuade the Christian to love him or her. The assumption here is that a Jew would never harm a Christian because "Jacob, was a mild man, who stayed in camp" (Genesis 25:27) and, therefore, presumably would not bite. Esau, by contrast, was considered the aggressive brother.

This perception has, alas, been borne out by history. During most of our common past, Christians have had access to power that they have used, and Jews have not. To this day, and despite protestations by many Christians, Jews see themselves as a hounded, persecuted minority living in a powerful and potentially dangerous Christian world. From the start, therefore, even those Jews who engage in

Christian-Jewish dialogue do not see the relationship as symmetrical. But, unlike other Jews, they hope it becomes so. It takes much effort to see myself as an equal partner in dialogue and not as an advocate for a minority. I am even uncomfortable writing this, because I fear many of my fellow Jews will criticize me, not necessarily because they disagree with my observations but out of fear that, through self-exposure, I am weakening the already weak and defensive Jewish position, and that Christians may take advantage of it.

My intention is, of course, very different. I wish to contribute to a debate that might help us find the proper level and framework for purposeful and mutually satisfying co-operation. I have positive reasons that motivate my involvement in Christian-Jewish dialogue. I view such involvement as an important source for my own religious life as a Jew. To gain access to that source, I have often distanced myself from fellow Jews whose enthusiasm for Christian-Jewish dialogue is limited to a desire to show Christians that Judaism is not what is being portrayed in their hostile literature but very similar to Christian ways.

That I am a Reform rabbi is relevant in this context. It is, of course, both historically and theologically inaccurate to accuse Reform Judaism of seeking to imitate Christianity, as many malicious Jewish opponents of Reform often do. Yet it is an inescapable fact that, because Reform in its outer manifestations is more accessible to non-Jews, some, perhaps many, Reform Jews have wanted their synagogues to create the "right" image of Judaism for their Christian neighbours. They invariably expect the rabbis to articulate and personify that image. A sign of success by which a Reform rabbi is often judged is the way in which he or she is viewed by Christian leaders.

Such inauthentic existence has its roots in anti-Semitism turned against itself and manifesting itself as Jewish self-hatred. In *Jewish Self-Hatred,* Sander L. Gilman shows how the persistence and intensity of anti-Semitism has made some Jews internalize its message and conclude that Jews are indeed what anti-Semites accuse them of being.[4] But those same Jews had to find a way of showing the anti-Semites that they were different, and, therefore, the castigation may apply to others but not to them. Hence the disdain, referred to in chapter 18, with which German Jews before Hitler treated recent arrivals from eastern Europe, the so-called *Ostjuden*. And, hence the original distance between the established Jews in Canada and the "greeners," the new immigrants. That is probably also why assimilated Jews so often are more preoccupied with anti-Semitism than others. And that is why the same Jews are so keen that their Christian neighbours think well of them.

This may help explain why many of those Jews involved in Jewish-Christian dialogue are assimilated and secular. I suspect that working for Jewish-Christian co-operation is one way to believe that they can be accepted by the majority Christian culture. That there is so little theological discussion in our encounters supports the suspicion. This situation may also account for the lack of progress. How can you bring the two religions closer when representatives of one may not believe in their own?

It is not surprising, therefore, that the many excellent organizations established to promote Jewish-Christian co-operation are starved for funds and ideas. They only thrive when there is something to be indignant about, like an outburst of overt anti-Semitic activity, preferably far away. By looking at things close to home, these organizations run the risk of upsetting the various establishments acting as their titular patrons. We are, therefore, confronted with the paradox that groups ostensibly dedicated to Christian-Jewish relations rarely engage in real dialogue and often refuse to confront burning issues.

Despite David Novak's attempt to offer a Jewish theological affirmation of the Christian-Jewish encounter, I find it difficult to be optimistic about it.[5] Novak's thesis is based on the common goal of redemption, despite the different tasks that Christians and Jews have been assigned in their respective covenants with God. However, if there are still exponents of Christianity who believe that the Jews delay redemption, Novak's optimistic perspective seems as remote as all the other efforts.

Even if few theologians pay attention to it, the masses will remain unaffected. Thus Abraham Brumberg, an expert on Polish affairs, challenges the existing opportunities for high-level dialogue between Christians and Jews because the outcome in no way affects attitudes at the grassroots. He writes: "The 'dialogue,' then, is not designed to have much, if any, impact on most Catholic believers. It is not brought down to the level of the parish pulpit."[6] If even the Church in Poland — where anti-Semitism led to genocide; where it is still a force even among the so-called progressives, and that despite the fact that Poland has become virtually *Judenrein;* and where the Church is extremely powerful — is not affected by dialogue, what hope is there anywhere else?

The conclusion one must come to, therefore, is that open, honest and comprehensive Christian-Jewish relations remain impossible. Judaism disappoints Christians while Christianity disappoints many Jews who hoped that the new era of religious tolerance and co-operation would bring the equality and symmetry they have dreamed of since the Enlightenment.

The pessimism among Jews is rooted in what Jews see as the Christians' failure to understand the significance of Israel for contemporary Jewish consciousness. When Cardinal Carter, the Catholic Archbishop of Toronto and a genuine friend of the Jewish people, declared that, although he could grasp intellectually the Jews' attachment to Israel he could not empathize with it emotionally,[7] the Jews who heard him were confused and disappointed. They asked: Did he really not understand, or was he merely pretending for reasons of politics and expediency? He did not know why they did not believe him. They could not understand how he failed to perceive the obvious.

Similarly, when the Conference of Catholic Bishops in Canada and the Toronto Conference of the United Church of Canada issued statements critical of Israeli policies, Jews understood the pronouncements to imply that the Israelis are the sole culprits in Middle Eastern conflicts. They regarded the statements as another manifestation of Christian anti-Semitism — this time in the guise of a perceived pro-Palestinian stance. I am inclined to accept the assurances of the authors of these statements that anti-Semitism is abhorrent to them, but that they seem unable to understand the true significance of Israel for contemporary Jewish consciousness. Those who opposed dialogue feel vindicated; those who had hoped for understanding feel let down. And when they say so, they run the risk of irritating their Christian friends.

Not all Jews think this way. Marc Ellis has written suggesting that Christian-Jewish dialogue has reached an impasse for reasons akin to those I have cited. But he then states that the only way out of that impasse is to acknowledge that what the Jewish people collectively now do to Palestinians is the same as what the Church has been doing to Jews through the ages. By urging the United States to stop supporting Israel, Christians would dissolve the "ecumenical bargain" by which they are expected by Jews to embrace the State of Israel.[8] That Ellis does not distinguish between the Jewish state and the government of that state is telling. I doubt if many Jews engaged in Christian-Jewish relations expect Christians to endorse the policies of Israel's government, but they do expect an understanding of the significance and centrality of Jewish statehood for Judaism today. Jewish sovereignty seems to Jews the only safeguard against anti-Semitism. A failure to recognize this amounts to implied encouragement and aid to the continued persecution of Jews.

I write as someone who has often been critical of Israeli government policies vis-à-vis the Palestinians, and as an advocate of Jewish withdrawal from the "territories" as the necessary condition for the establishment of Palestinian sovereignty. I believe that Jewish settlements on the West Bank and in Gaza, whether legally justified and strategically advantageous or not, are a provocation. Yet, to see Israeli government action in the last years or decades as equivalent to the Church's action against the Jewish people over the centuries is a disturbing distortion of history. If the only way of creating a symmetry in Jewish-Christian dialogue is for Jews to pronounce themselves as culpable as the Christian Church, then the dialogue has not merely reached an impasse, but it is dead — and people like Ellis are helping bury it in the guise of wishing to revive it.

The two cardinal issues in contemporary Jewish life are the Holocaust and the State of Israel. Jews feel misunderstood by Christians on both. As a result, the more we talk, the less we say to each other; the more we insist that times have changed, the more they seem to be the same.

Yet for all my pessimism, I want to help promote Christian-Jewish co-operation. I teach a class for Christian theology students on contemporary Jewish thought. I have hosted Archbishop Desmond

Tutu and would do so again, despite my disagreement with him over Israel. I am also involved in many other projects to further Jewish-Christian understanding. If things are so bad, why are they so good? Let me attempt a personal answer.

The possibility of creating a climate of understanding between Christians and Jews through their official and authorized representatives seems remote. But the opportunities for individual Jews and Christians to be spiritually enriched by encountering each other in this open society are enormous. Official Christian-Jewish encounters yield few results, but Christian-Jewish dialogue works between individuals. While Churches will continue to make statements about Israel that Jews will see as hostile, individual Christians exist who not only understand the significance of statehood for Judaism, but can share the pains and ambiguities that contemporary political realities have imposed on Jews. Cardinal Carter, a prince of the Church, may not understand the significance of Israel for Jews, but Walter Brueggemann, a Bible scholar and Christian theologian, does.[9] Similarly, some Christians can rise above the theological presuppositions that Jews should forgive the Nazis, without compromising their own Christian commitment. The same people can also see the damage caused by an unbalanced statement on Israel, an unguarded comment on the Holocaust or an unwarranted threat against those who object to tourism to Oberammergau, where the intensely anti-Jewish passion play has been performed.

There are Jews who engage in Jewish-Christian dialogue, not because they naively believe they will cure anti-Semitism, but because it deepens their own religious commitment, not in a vain attempt to make a good impression, but out of an earnest resolve to affirm other believers. They do not pretend to have reached complete agreement, but they sense that they walk in the same direction and need each other's support.

Christian-Jewish encounters will not rewrite history, compensate for past sins or blur theological differences. Dialogue seems to work, however, when one believer reveals herself or himself to another believer and thus validates the conviction that there are other paths to God.

Religious encounters with Christians have a similar effect on me as the encounter with Eugene Rosenstock had on the young Franz Rosenzweig in 1913.[10] Rosenzweig was so impressed by Rosenstock's Christian convictions that he went back to study his own tradition and, as a result, came to formulate Judaism in a new key. I do not aspire to the insights of a genius, but I do aspire to the commitment and enthusiasm of a Jew who has found his Jewish path with the help of many, some of whom are committed Christians.

It is Rosenzweig's contemporary and collaborator, Martin Buber, who through his philosophy of dialogue has enabled me to understand how such help works. As Buber might have put it: As Jews we may be neurotic and prejudiced; as Christians you may be burdened by a history, a hierarchy and a theology; but what happens between us can be real, manifest as the work of the *Shechina,* 'the presence of God' by whatever name we may wish to call it. My involvement in Jewish-Christian co-operation has helped shape my own conviction that, as much as we may need institutions, and as much as I am part of several of them, the spirit of God is most discernible in individuals, no matter what institutions or religious traditions they belong to. Since these individuals are invariably in a minority, they need each other for comfort and strength. Marilyn Ferguson, quoted in chapter 10, calls such people conspirators, men and women who recognize the advent of a new paradigm and are prepared to advance its course ahead of others, although the majority continues to defend the old. Christian-Jewish dialogue is most effective when it becomes a forum for such conspirators, not to take cover in the face of a common enemy, but to blaze a trail in search of a common destiny.

Some people justify Christian-Jewish dialogue by suggesting that the time has come for Jews and Christians to stop arguing with each other because contemporary history demands that they join to fight their ever-more potent enemy, secularism. It is doubtful whether such a cynical call for an uneasy alliance is possible or helpful. It may not be possible, because it ignores the fact that one difference between Judaism and Christianity is their respective attitudes to secularism. And that one thing we can learn from each other is how to accommodate ourselves to the secular civil religion of our time.

The call to fight the alleged enemy may not be helpful, because it suggests that only foes can forge friendship between us. The call to arms against a common enemy can be a reflection of spiritual bankruptcy. The call to fight secularism through Christian-Jewish dialogue seems a way of transposing the earlier call to fight anti-Semitism through Christian-Jewish encounters. Since secularism is not going to be defeated in this way, just as Christian-Jewish relations have not defeated anti-Semitism, the enterprise seems doomed to failure.

If the biblical Jacob is identified with the Jewish people and his brother Esau with gentiles, the possibility of a genuine embrace must be questioned. But if Jacob and Esau are seen in the way the Bible describes them, as two individuals with a common ancestry but a different history, an embrace becomes possible each time individuals meet. The conflict posed at the beginning of this chapter can be resolved in typical rabbinic fashion. Those who say Esau bit Jacob, have an abstract collective in mind. Those who testify to a genuine embrace and a genuine kiss, have individuals in mind.

I began by suggesting that nothing has changed since the time of the rabbinic exegesis. Let me modify that and say that the only prospect for change is greater emphasis on individual encounters and an ever-widening circle of "conspirators," caused by the open society in which we live, and the liberal ambiance in which we work. Eventually, this stance may become the norm rather than the exception.

Most of the traditional and statutory organizations and committees set up to bring the Jewish people and the Christian church closer together are languishing. Individual efforts, however, continue to flourish. I never cease to be enriched by frequent contacts with fellow-"conspirators" who do not seek to deny history or rewrite theology, but who try to learn from one another and, through creative synthesis, deepen their own religious commitment with the help of the insights and the experiences of the other.

Only when we have realized the futility of adjusting theology for the sake of making a good impression, and only when we have accepted that the past cannot be altered, does real Christian-Jewish dialogue become possible. Only when Jacob remains Jacob with all his foibles and feelings, and Esau is Esau without denying his stance, can they embrace as brothers. When they attempt more, Esau's kiss turns into a bite and Jacob's neck turns to marble so that Esau breaks his teeth.[11] Let our dialogue always leave us with open arms and unbroken teeth.

Notes

1 The Masoretic text is the vocalized text of the Hebrew Bible used in all standard editions.

2 Rashi on Genesis 33:4.

3 R. Yannai in Genesis Rabba 78:12.

4 Sander L. Gilman, *Jewish Self-Hatred: Anti-Semitism and the Hidden Language of the Jews* (Baltimore: The John Hopkins University Press, 1986).

5 David Novak, *Jewish-Christian Dialogue: A Jewish Justification* (Oxford: Oxford University Press, 1989).

6 Abraham Brumberg, "The Problem That Won't Go Away: Anti-Semitism in Poland (Again)," *Tikkun* (January/February, 1990): 33.

7 In a lecture at Holy Blossom Temple, Toronto, on November 27, 1989.

8 Marc Ellis, "Jewish-Christian Impasse," *The Tablet* (January 20, 1990): 71ff.

9 See Brueggemann's *The Land* (Philadelphia: Fortress Press, 1977).

10 See, for example, Nahum N. Glatzer, *Franz Rosenzweig: His Life and Thought* (New York: Schocken, 1961), 23ff.

11 Genesis Rabba 78:12.

20

Christians and Jews
After the Holocaust

September 1, 1939 marks the beginning of my anxiety neurosis. I was four years old when the Germans invaded my native Poland and shattered the world of my middle-class childhood. My parents and I fled our hometown that day, and I have been "on the run" ever since. The 50th anniversary of that fateful day speaks to me personally, and I can reflect on it only in a personal way.

One of the many lessons I have learned in the last 50 years is that nothing Jews do seems to help eradicate, or even diminish, anti-Semitism. The many organizations seeking to foster Christian-Jewish understanding by educating the masses usually have an impact only on those who do not need it. That is, on men and women who often, through self-scrutiny, had already come to the conclusion that hatred is a much greater burden for the hater than for the hated, although the latter are the victims who suffer the physical consequences.

The Christian and Jewish establishments that support such efforts are trying to come to terms with their own unease by pretending something is being done. That is why work in the field of Jewish-Christian understanding has had so little impact at the grassroots.

Reprinted from *Compass* (November 1989).

I am sure that most, if not all, Christians would like to eradicate anti-Semitism, but they may very well have come to the conclusion that it can be done only by eradicating Judaism, or, at least, all Jews. That many Jews seem to be secular is viewed with considerable enthusiasm in many circles, because it appears to provide opportunities for Christian missionary activity. The passionate Zionism of many Christian evangelicals is an even more serious threat. It supports the return of the Jews to their own land in the hope that, once they are together in one place, they will embrace Christianity. In this way, Jewish and Christian messianic expectations will converge and be consummated. Our "friends" seem to display love for us while showing hatred for who we are.

Seen from this perspective, the Holocaust is "only" a secularized and unspeakably brutal attempt to get rid of anti-Semitism by getting rid of the Jews: the final solution. Many thoughtful Christians recognized the roots of Nazism in Christianity and were horrified. They tried to alert fellow Christians to the painful truth that anti-Semitism was not the Jews' problem, but their own, and that they had to do something about it. Many listened and some acted. But have the churches changed sufficiently to accommodate their insights?

Because I must find a resting place — some assurance that the homelessness of the last 50 years is over — I must believe that ours is, at least potentially, a better world, and that the new relationship between Christianity and Judaism epitomizes it. That is why I am trying to be a liberal. Yet despite my need to believe the best, I have doubts. That could be because of my neurosis. But then, it could also be because of factual, objective evidence.

In the Middle Ages, some Jewish men of substance played the role of go-betweens, or *shtadlanim,* with easy access to the king and, at times, even the bishop. My fellow Jews, who today still like to act as *shtadlanim,* assure me that much has changed in Jewish-Christian relations. They point to secret negotiations, friendships and the occasional public statement. I hope they are right, but I remain unconvinced. It all seems so medieval, so very much the same as it has always been between Christians and Jews.

My scepticism is linked to my suspicion of all secret negotiations, especially between exponents of religious traditions. We are, after all, not negotiating treaties but examining our hearts and minds. Surely, that is possible only in open debate.

If I remain actively involved in work for Jewish-Christian understanding, it is not because I believe we can trust each other, but because I believe that despite the obstacles, we must work towards such trust. I also have two specific reasons to be involved.

First, I very much want Christianity to be free of Jew-hatred. Since I do not believe I can do anything to make Christians change their minds collectively, I am most eager to support those who wish to testify to their commitment to the truth about Jews and Judaism amid the lies that have created the climate of hate.

The second reason for my need to work with Christians springs from my understanding of the challenge of contemporary Judaism. During the first two decades after the Holocaust, I was moved by the survivors from the death camps who told us that silence was the only legitimate response to the tragedy. In the decade that followed, and especially after the Six Day War, I realized that survival was our primary aim as Jews. I was moved by Emil Fackenheim's charge not to give Hitler his posthumous victory by going under. But, in 1982, I published *Beyond Survival.* In that book, I tried to express the need to formulate Judaism positively, as purposeful, not only in the negatively defiant manner implied in the quest for survival.

Part of that Jewish purpose is reflected in solidarity: because Jews have suffered at the hands of tyrants, we must survive to identify with those who suffer, wherever and whoever they may be, and to seek to alleviate their suffering. This is a modern reformulation of the biblical injunction to love the stranger "because you were strangers in the land of Egypt" (Leviticus 19:34).

The religious world is increasingly inhospitable to liberal ideas and to solidarity with the oppressed. Therefore, those with different religious traditions who hold such ideas must be close to one another, so our testimony survives and our actions are not proven quixotic.

My dual need to co-operate with Christians brings me to a tentative conclusion. We will never be able to fully fathom the past, let alone eradicate the scars it has inflicted. But we may be able to identify areas of consensus and co-operation and, through common endeavour, build a climate of trust. While this will not alter the past, it may prevent its repetition.

Judaism is about more than survival, but it can never be about less. And Jewish survival after the Holocaust is unthinkable without Jewish sovereignty, which means the State of Israel. Even the vastly improved conditions of Jews in the western Diaspora are due more to Jewish self-confidence — the knowledge that we always have a home in Israel — than to the magnanimity and tolerance of the societies in which we live. Israel is crucial to Jewish continuity everywhere.

It is also essential for the realization of Jewish purpose inherent in solidarity. We must be strong and secure to help the weak and the hounded. If we take seriously the prophet's charge to be "a light unto the nations" (Isaiah 51:4), we must have full access to our own source of spiritual and physical energy. Israel is precisely that.

Therefore, it is wrong to view the establishment of the Jewish state as a consolation prize for the Holocaust. The land of Israel has always been at the centre of Jewish life and Jewish consciousness, whether Jews had access to it or not. The Holocaust merely proved the tragic truth that every attempt by Jews to find the Promised Land elsewhere was a mistake. Anti-Semitism may be the problem of the gentiles, but because Jews are the victims, they were forced to take steps to emerge from powerlessness and return to history.

21

With Christians in Israel

I attended recently a very special worship service. The setting was the spot on Lake Kinneret (the Sea of Galilee) where, according to Christian tradition, Jesus performed the miracle of the loaves and fishes that provided food for thousands. The occasion was a Christian Communion Service: the group of some 50 Christians, with whom I had the honour of travelling to Israel, was celebrating this most sacred act in the Christian liturgy.

Most participants were moved to tears. I was deeply touched by seeing my friends so affected.

This memorable half-hour, on a glorious Sunday morning, helped me crystallize my understanding of what Israel means to believing Christians. The tour — the pilgrimage — had a deep effect and a lasting impact on the lives of many. But it was a different impact from what I have seen when travelling with groups of Jews. For Jews, Israel is about our history, our family — our people; but for Christians, Israel is about Jesus — their faith.

It was a new perspective on Israel for me. On some 20 previous visits I had seen Israel from many angles, but never from this one. I am, therefore, most grateful to Reverend Dr. Stanford Lucyk for making me the "Jewish resource person" on this tour, devised, planned, organized and most-admirably conducted by him.

Originally delivered, in 1986, as a sermon at Holy Blossom Temple and subsequently published in the magazine of the Timothy Eaton Memorial Church in Toronto under the title, " 'My Country' with Canadian Christians: A Rabbi's Perspective."

Jews believe that only their appreciation of Israel is true and authentic, so it was sobering to view the country differently. I returned even more in love with, and committed to, Israel because of this experience.

Perhaps the best way in which I can convey differences in perception is by reporting on three incidents.

On a visit to the Golan Heights, our guide explained the strategic significance of the region. He told us how Israeli settlements farther south could live in safety because, during the Six Day War, the Syrians were pushed back beyond the hills that overlook Israeli territory. Again, it was a glorious day and we enjoyed the scenery, the wildflowers and the interesting sites. Suddenly our bus stopped for a convoy of Israeli tanks. A respectful silence fell on the bus. After all, here was the military. We sat patiently and waited until the road was clear.

I was thinking how differently a Jewish group would have reacted. They would have insisted on getting out of the bus and would have wanted to climb on the tanks and be photographed with the officers. For Jews, these tanks represent *bittachon*, 'security'; for non-Jews they are the deadly weapons of a world-famous army.

This latter reaction is natural. It is also shared by many Israelis who are more cautious about the military than they were in the early days of the state. The war with Lebanon changed so many perceptions. I was grateful for the reserve of my companions. It served as a welcome corrective to my own, perhaps outmoded, romantic Zionist euphoria at the sight of Jewish power.

The second incident occurred during our tour to Bethlehem, a town not normally on the itinerary of Jewish groups. I had only visited the place once and briefly. On this occasion, the visit was extensive and included a meeting with the town's world-famous mayor, Elias Freij.

Now it was my turn to be reserved. As he explained his precarious position as a Christian mayor of a half-Christian and half-Muslim Arab town "under occupation," I was more sceptical and felt he made more of an impression on the group than on me.

I understand why Christians reacted differently. After all, they were in the company of a fellow-believer; I was in the presence of a potential enemy. And I am not sure that their views are not more legitimate and helpful than my fears and my reserve. I came away strengthened in my resolve to learn to trust more, especially when it is so difficult.

No visit to Israel is possible without going to Yad Vashem, the Holocaust memorial in Jerusalem. Many members of the group felt distinctly uncomfortable: vaguely responsible but not at all guilty. They would have probably argued that it was necessary for them to go to Yad Vashem, but they did not know how to react to the visit. I tried to explain the Jewish perspective, but I realized there was a gulf between us. For me, the memorial was to my family, my people. For them, it marked a period in history, far away in time and space and best forgotten.

It cannot be otherwise. I realized this a day or so later when we visited the Armenian compound in Jerusalem. The bishop who showed us around referred to the massacre of two million Armenians by the Turks. Of course, I knew about it, but for me that was history, whereas for him it was biography. It is impossible to feel another person's pain, however hard one tries.

These three incidents illustrate three central issues in contemporary Israel: defence and the pre-occupation with survival; the West Bank and the implications for Jewish-Arab relations; and the Holocaust and the need to make sure that it does not happen again. On all three, Jews and Christians are bound to have different perceptions. Before we decide who is right and who is wrong, let us learn from one another.

There might have been a fourth experience, illustrating a fourth aspect of Israeli concern: religious diversity. I had hoped to take the group on a walking tour through Meah Shearim, Jerusalem's ultra-Orthodox quarter. But I was advised against it. The growing militancy among Orthodox extremists makes walking with large groups unsafe.

You may ask what I was doing on this trip, despite my lofty title. It is a legitimate question to which I do not know the full answer. But I do know my presence was appreciated and I was most grateful to have been included. On reflection, perhaps I acted as a kind of host. Many participants spoke to me about Israel as "your country."

Perhaps some of you might have been offended by this. I was not. On the contrary. It felt like my country more than it had ever done before, even if this feeling only accentuates the dilemma of the Diaspora Jew: an outsider in his or her own country and not really at home in Israel.

A second role might have been that of witness. I was obviously not involved in the Communion Service, but I witnessed it. I was moved when a Lutheran pastor from Detroit interpreted the miracle of feeding the people as a charge on all those present to feed others with the experience of Israel, the old and the new. And I was moved when Canon Borden Purcell [at the time Chairperson of the Ontario Human Rights Commission] prayed for the speedy release from the Soviet Union of Jews who wish to leave. Purcell and Lucyk had visited refuseniks in the Soviet Union; this was a continuation of their pilgrimage.

A few weeks ago, I heard Dr. David Hartman, the distinguished Jewish thinker, speak in Toronto about how much more universalist he had become once he moved to Israel. Being surrounded by Jewish particularism in the Jewish state, he could be open to "the world," thus stressing the universalist dimension of Judaism. Travelling in "my country" with Canadian Christians, I had moments of the same feeling, for which I am immensely grateful.

Confessions

This concluding section doesn't really belong in this volume, for most of it is personal, almost private. Yet that is why it has been included.

The 25 essays collected here have been selected as representative of ideas to which members of Holy Blossom Temple and others have been exposed in my first 10 years as the congregation's senior rabbi. It is, therefore, only right and proper that readers know something about the man who has written and spoken the words.

The late Rabbi Leo Baeck, the great exponent of liberal Judaism and legendary leader of German Jewry during the Nazi period, is said to have never used the first person singular in public. He wanted his ideas to speak for themselves. Though I have not imposed on myself the same discipline, I have probably been less personal than many of my rabbinic colleagues. My aim has been to convey a message without clouding it with autobiography.

This is an attempt to make up for it. Yet, I have rejected the editors' suggestion to place this section at the beginning of the book. *What* is being said must take precedence over *who* says it, even though the background and experiences of the author have, of course, a bearing on each of the texts. Should the reader now wish to go back to any of the chapters in the previous five sections, the "revelations" of the sixth may shed some new light on them.

22

How I Found Faith

Ove Nordstrandh was an ordained Minister in the Church of Sweden and a Doctor of Theology, who taught religious studies in Gothenburg. I have not spoken to him since I left the city in 1955. But I think of him often, for he, probably more than any other person, is responsible for my taking religion seriously enough to become a rabbi.

The Sweden in which I grew up was, spiritually, a very polarized country. Religious people were other-worldly and deadly serious; their dress and manner were invariably dull, for drabness was considered a sign of piety. I never saw any religious person I knew in those days laugh. By contrast, the secularists were "free"; to them nothing was sacred, except sex perhaps, for this was the era of the early Ingmar Bergman films.

I did not belong to either group. First, because I was a Jew and, therefore, by the rules of Swedish society, an outsider. Second, because my particular background made me neither free enough to be a secularist nor pious enough to be a religionist.

But Nordstrandh was different. He looked like a secularist and talked like a religious person. He spoke of God and laughed a lot. I had never met anybody like him before, and I was enchanted. So it was possible to be religious *and* ordinary at the same time! Perhaps those feelings and thoughts I had about religion could be combined with normal existence, after all. I began to understand that "religion" and "piety" were not synonymous.

Address to the Etobicoke Ecumenical Fellowship, February 5, 1991.

My teacher must have sensed my interest, for he gave me a special project. I was to write an essay on the essence of Judaism. It was the first time in my life that I had studied the subject seriously. He was pleased with the result and I got top marks. This was very important to a refugee boy of 18, anxious to rise from squalor and poverty by doing well at school.

To balance my non-Jewish environment of school and society, I was active in the small Jewish community in Gothenburg. The summer after I did my project on Judaism, for example, I was involved in running the annual summer camp for Jewish youth in Scandinavia.

There, I met Fredzia Zonabend a girl from Stockholm. We got talking, and before the week-long camp was over, I proposed — and she accepted. We married two years later. I had mentioned to her that I wanted to be a rabbi, and she was enthusiastic. However, it was not only her enthusiasm that gave me courage, it was much more her love. Years later, when I read Martin Buber, I realized why it is impossible to love God without loving another human being. Hebrew has the same word for love of God and love of neighbour. The bifurcation between *agape* and *eros* is unknown in Judaism.

I did nothing to find out how one becomes a rabbi. There were other things I had to do first. For example, I had to find a job so I could get married. I decided to move to Stockholm when I finished school.

The night before I left Gothenburg, there was a meeting in the Jewish Community Centre that I was asked to chair, as a farewell gesture. One of those present was the new rabbi. After the meeting, he said to me, "Have you thought of becoming a rabbi?" He helped me to make the final decision; he also told me how to apply for grants.

I now had the motivation and the encouragement. But I still did not know much about faith, in general, or Judaism, in particular. For my upbringing had been complicated by the Second World War. I was four when Hitler invaded my native Poland in 1939, and my family fled East. During the war, there was little time for education or religious life. My most persistent memory of those years is of being hungry. When we returned to Poland in 1946, all we found were ruins and anti-Semitism. The hatred of Jews was so strong that my parents did not dare to send me to a Polish school. Instead I went to a small Hebrew-speaking school that prepared children to settle in Israel.

One day, I heard that the parents of a friend at school had arranged with the local rabbi for the boy's Bar Mitzvah. I decided to do the same. Realizing my parents had no interest in such things, I arranged it myself. War children grow up quickly and get along with as little parental support as possible. When the day came, my father came to the synagogue; my mother saw no reason for doing so. In his later years, my father became a regular worshipper in the synagogue in Gothenburg until his death in 1973; my mother continues the tradition to this very day.

I recall vividly the conversation between my father and the rabbi on the day of my Bar Mitzvah. "This boy," the rabbi said with a smile, "will one day be a rabbi." Everybody got the joke and laughed heartily, or as heartily as Jews laughed in Poland in the winter of 1948. The same rabbi later moved to Israel, where he became known as a sage and clairvoyant. Though I was far removed from his extreme Orthodox world, he knew I had, indeed, become a Reform rabbi. However, I do not think he was particularly proud of his prophecy; he mentioned it to no one.

My religious upbringing was virtually non-existent. But I did know Hebrew. Thanks to that, I was offered a job as the assistant to the cultural counsellor at the Israeli embassy in Stockholm. I owe much to the two years I spent there. They not only enabled Fredzia and me to get married, but they made me painfully aware of how ignorant I was of Judaism.

After our first visit to Israel in the spring of 1957, I quit my job at the embassy and enrolled as a rabbinic student at the Leo Baeck College in London. It was not a sudden conversion that took me there; in fact, Judaism does not know of such things. I got to rabbinic school because of many people: the Swedish theologian, the new rabbi in Gothenburg and my boss at the embassy in Stockholm, a well-known Israeli writer and a disciple of the Chasidic school of Nachman of Bratslav. But, above all, it was because of my wife.

I have a cartoon in my office that says, "Religion is not a product." The other day I had reason to tell someone who was describing how to market Judaism that religion is a disease you catch, not a commodity you sell or buy. I never bought Judaism, but I did catch it from several people — Jews and non-Jews. I have already mentioned my Christian teacher. Let me now add a distinguished western Buddhist: the late Dr. Edward Conze, author of books on Buddhism that are still in print. I attended his lectures in London more than 30 years ago; they had a great impact on me.

I entered rabbinic school as a searching Jew; it was a nameless need for direction in life and the quest for knowledge that brought me there. To become a believing Jew took longer. It came about through some of my teachers and thanks to many books. Were I to mention only one book, apart from the Bible and the other sacred texts, it would be Martin Buber's *I and Thou.* But, above all, I became a believing Jew when I became a father. We had lost three babies in stillbirths before our first child was born. We experienced the arrival of our daughter as a miracle. The subsequent arrival of her brother and sister further confirmed it. I now could understand why the biblical matriarchs had such difficulties having children: it was yet another way in which Scripture tells us that life is a gift, not an entitlement.

I could now begin to understand what God must be like. God is described in Jewish tradition as *harachaman,* 'the Merciful One,' a term also used by Muslims. The word is the same as the Hebrew *rechem,* 'womb.' God's love is the same as a mother feels for her child. I have always, only half in jest, described myself as a Jewish mother.

The fact that Judaism is family-centred is not only a matter of psychology and sociology; it is a theological category, and that is how I experienced it. God is described as a parent and as a spouse in our literature. It is only thanks to my family that I have begun to fathom the meaning of terms such as love, obligation, trust, grace, forgiveness, hope and the rest of the theological vocabulary. That is probably also why I became a marriage therapist a few years after I became a rabbi; the two occupations seem rooted in the same value system.

All this is fine, but why a rabbi? My parents were, of course, opposed to my choice of profession, not only because as ardent socialists, they saw religion as the opiate of the people, but because they wanted me to have a "respectable" profession. Yet it was not rebellion that made me go against my parents' wishes.

What was it, then? I am still not sure, but I suspect that it is the guilt of the survivor.

My wife and I are rare species of our generation: we survived the Holocaust as children — she in the ghetto of Lodz and the concentration camp of Ravensbrueck; I in Siberia and the Soviet Republic of Uzbekistan. Although we could not articulate it then, in retrospect I think that, from the moment we met, we were searching for an answer to the question, "Why did we survive?" To serve our people seemed the most obvious response. And out of that service, coupled with personal experiences, we have come to serve God together.

That service is born out of human love and what Jewish tradition calls *yirat shamayim,* 'the fear of heaven,' which means the recognition of God's power over our lives. I stand in awe, even in fear, before that power, ready to offer my version of the prophet's response when he said, *hineni,* 'here I am.'

23

How I Became a Rabbi

I became a rabbi in July, 1962. The event came as a shock to my teachers at Leo Baeck College in London, where I had studied for five years, and as an anti-climax to me.

A shock because the College was obviously totally unprepared for the event. Although I was not the first student to enter, I was the first to go through the full course and qualify. This made me the first student to be subjected to an examination — and nobody was quite prepared for it.

The anti-climax was because of that unpreparedness. My final oral examination was an embarrassment because during it two lecturers quarrelled over a biblical passage. The next day, a teacher set me an impossible task — to settle an old score — which prompted even the director, normally not one of my advocates, to intervene on my behalf. That it took another couple of years before I was given a diploma — and then another few years before I received the printed document — further added to my dissatisfaction.

I learned much in the five years. But had I depended only on what I had been taught, I would have been totally unprepared for the practical rabbinate. The college saw itself as an academic institution, which meant that it provided little vocational training. I recall only a class in elocution, intended primarily for students from Britain who might wish to polish their "working-class" accents. As a

Reprinted from *Manna* (Winter 1988), where it appeared under the title, "How Not to Kiss Babies — And Love the Rabbinate."

foreigner with idiosyncratic ways of butchering the English tongue, I was apparently beyond redemption. After all, most of the teachers, immigrants from other countries, did not speak the Queen's English either. Having a foreigner in their midst gave them some confidence.

And they needed all the confidence they could get. Their only model was the Hochschule fuer die Wissenschaft des Judentums, in Berlin where they had studied. During the almost two decades between the closure of the Hochschule and the opening of the Leo Baeck College, most of them had had little contact with academic institutions. This made them nervous and defensive.

Because I was disappointed — for I had come from Sweden hoping to find a small, but established college — I was unduly aggressive. Moreover, I was not being financed by the British Reform movement, which had established the college and, therefore, could go somewhere else, which I threatened to do often. Since, for a while I was the only bona fide student, it was important for the college that I stay. The insecurity of its leadership in the face of my rebelliousness did not make for a happy relationship. Even the more than three decades have not quite removed the bitter taste in my mouth.

If I persevered, it was thanks to one man only: the late Dr. Ignaz Maybaum. He took a liking to me, which could not have been easy, and found work for me in his congregation, the Edgware and District Reform Synagogue. I learned from Maybaum what it means to be a rabbi in a Reform congregation — and to enjoy it. He has remained the most important influence in my life, as a man and as a teacher. In spite of his trials and tribulations — and an inadequate salary — he loved the congregation and taught me to love all Jews.

That love was strong enough to help me survive my student pulpit. I find it difficult to look back on the couple of years I spent there without disdain. True, I was new, young and inexperienced. But that did not entitle the leadership to take such full advantage of me. In the end, I was rescued not by the college but by my physician, who insisted that the congregation was injurious to my health and provided the necessary documentation. The certificate did not endear me to the leadership of the college but it let me off and I survived, literally.

What made me flourish, was my first full-time pulpit, the South-West Essex Reform Synagogue in Ilford. Its rabbi, Dr. Alan W. Miller, had left for the United States in the autumn of 1961 and since I was "too sick" to travel to my student pulpit, I was sent to conduct services at South-West Essex. It was love at first sight. Although I still had more than six months before graduating, I was offered the post on my first visit.

I wanted to accept but, since I had been sponsored by the Jewish community in Stockholm with a view to returning to Sweden, I wrote to ask what they had in mind for me. They prevaricated, perhaps fearing I was using the offer to put pressure on them. To give them time, I accepted South-West Essex for an initial year — and spent seven very happy years there. The congregation has remained "the love of my youth."

What the college could not do in five years, the South-West Essex Reform Synagogue did in a few months. It taught me to love the rabbinate. I cannot think of any other work that I would rather do in life.

The members of the Synagogue did not describe themselves as intellectuals, but — largely thanks to my illustrious predecessor — they recognized that the primary task of the rabbi is to teach Torah. The sermon became an important vehicle for that. I preached twice a week and was expected to say something. Therefore, it was assumed I would study. They also wanted me to teach children and adults, and this has remained my pattern in the rabbinate.

I gained so much confidence in my first full-time congregation that, even when I came to my next pulpit — the North Western Reform Synagogue in Golders Green — I had enough stamina to persevere and to cope with the adversity to which most new rabbis are subjected. My patience was vindicated; otherwise I could not have stayed there for 14 years.

It was the opportunity to do more of the same that took me to Canada. A colleague in England who, quite rightly, thought I was not qualified for the pulpit of Holy Blossom Temple in Toronto, shared his opinion that I was invited because they needed an administrator and did not want to pay much. On that score he was wrong. They wanted a teacher and felt that I might meet their needs.

Which brings me to my tribute to Leo Baeck College. My five years there may have been less than happy and my final examination less than memorable. But I did learn to love Torah, to respect learning and to enjoy teaching. The college may have ill-equipped me for the practical rabbinate, but it gave me enough direction and perseverance to teach with confidence, even in the face of adversity. And for that I am most grateful.

In the last quarter of a century, Leo Baeck College has seen many changes. I had a hand in one of them: greater emphasis on vocational training. I hope, however, that the initial stress on competence and familiarity with Hebrew texts, even if the student's English is less than idiomatic, has not been lost.

It is perhaps this advantage that Leo Baeck College has over its American big sister institution, the Hebrew Union College. The resources of the latter are infinitely greater, as are the opportunities for scholarship and excellence. Yet, as a product of Leo Baeck College, though deprived in many important respects, I also feel uniquely privileged to have been instilled with the belief that a rabbi is a teacher, not a salesperson, and that preaching matters at least as much as smiling.

The college did not teach me how to kiss babies at random in the community, and I am still deficient in that art. But it taught me how to handle texts and read books. It taught me the importance of ideas and the necessity of transmitting them. For all that I am deeply grateful. The gratitude outweighs the resentment — at least with the benefit of hindsight.

24

Sermons:
The Case for the Defence

Trying to mix Torah with sarcasm, the late Kurt Wilhelm, Chief Rabbi of Stockholm, once told me that the opposites listed in the third chapter of Ecclesiastes — "a time to be born and a time to die; a time to plant and a time to uproot" and so on — leave no room for alternatives. But there is one exception: "a time for silence and a time for speaking"; the alternative, or the compromise, to that is — preaching. The sermon, he concluded, in a self-deprecating manner so characteristic of disillusioned clergy, is not speech or silence but, presumably, incoherent noise, meaningless religio-babble.

Many congregants would agree. Often, they would much rather be left wondering why their rabbi did not remain silent instead of being left baffled because he did speak. And they have no inhibitions about expressing their views. If someone tells a rabbi that he or she actually stayed awake during the sermon, it is intended as a compliment.

Sometimes the criticism is even more explicit. I have actually asked people how they would feel if someone offered them the unsolicited testimonial that they were bad at their job and boring. They invariably respond that they would be deeply hurt. Yet they

Reprinted from *Viewpoints* 17:3 (1989). The piece was written soon after the publication of my volume of sermons, *Walking Toward Elijah* (Burlington, Ontario: Welch Publishing Company Inc., 1988).

were totally surprised that a rabbi should feel that way. They had assumed that standing in a pulpit must be such a privilege that the abuse received because of it was an insignificant price to pay. Most Jews believe rabbis, as public figures, are fair game, which may be one reason why sermons are so often attacked. Listeners are envious of preachers. They resent the perceived power of the pulpit, especially since they see themselves as part of a "captive" audience. Therefore, they lash out.

Not all do it openly; many choose more subtle methods. The sermon was sincere, they say, and, of course, the rabbi is free to say what he, or she, wants, *but*: this was not appropriate for the occasion; or it was too learned so that *they* (always the others) could not understand it; or it was too simplistic; or it was too long; or it was too short; and so on. The definition of a rabbi as "invisible six days of the week and incomprehensible on the seventh" has permeated our consciousness.

It has also intimidated rabbis. As a result, many are afraid to preach and believe that inventing alternatives shows their ability to be modern communicators. When they feel they must preach, on High Holy Days for example, they say the obvious to elicit approval —and, by implication, prove the charge of being boring. By enabling members of the congregation, especially its leaders, to hear what they want to hear, co-existence becomes possible. I doubt if any rabbi has ever lost his or her job for being boring.

Envy is, of course, not the only reason why sermons are usually so badly received. A more serious cause is the chasm between the nature of the message and the state of most contemporary Jews. They are often alienated from the tenets of Judaism and, therefore, find most statements about their religious heritage incomprehensible, if not offensive. Preacher and congregation literally do not speak the same language, although they use the same words. Since people do not like to admit their inability to grasp the content, they tend to blame the preacher for his or her style. Envy of the power of preaching is thus fused with hostility to the message.

That hostility has its roots in civil religion, the prevalent faith of our time. Jonathan Woocher's penetrating description and analysis of American civil Judaism, discussed earlier in chapter 3, sheds some light on our subject. Describing the difference between traditional religion and civil religion, Woocher says "civil religion's focus and locus is in the civilized political institutions of the community, not in the conventionally religious realm." As a result, "the prime bearers of civil religion are thus not . . . clergy or religious institutions, but the institution of polity itself and political leaders."[1]

One manifestation of the hostility to preachers is the perception that what is being said from the pulpit is irrelevant to contemporary Jewish life. If preachers want to be relevant, they are expected to deliver political sermons. The most successful of these are the ones that repeat what congregants have read in quality newspapers. What Torah is to the Jewish faith, the press is to Jewish civil religion.

A second feature of the difference between traditional and civil religion, according to Woocher, is that the former reaches to embrace the totality of human existence and of life's concerns, whereas the latter "seeks to embrace only that part of life which is public." As a result, "it can integrate individuals and groups with diverse personal beliefs and tolerate the existence of alternative meaning systems."[2]

This may explain why the same people who complain about the rabbi's boring sermons, also plead, in the most complimentary terms, to have the rabbi name their child or officiate at a family wedding or a Bar or Bat Mitzvah. It is public, theological pronouncements that Jews cannot stomach; they love and want personal ministrations. They believe traditional religion meets individual needs, while the collective expressions of Jewishness are taken care of by the civil religion. People may vilify the community rabbi, but they crave for the personal chaplain; while they criticize the sermons, they praise the eulogies. The same preaching style that was so irritating in the pulpit, becomes pleasing and meaningful in the funeral chapel or under the *chuppah*.

Besides the perceived "pulpit envy" and the hostility that is a function of the civil agenda of contemporary Jewry, two other reasons should be mentioned when discussing the decline of the sermon: the retreat of Christian influence on Jews and the impact of television and film.

When, for the first hundred years of its existence, the Reform Synagogue stressed the importance of preaching, and forced other movements to follow, it was, at least in part, an attempt to imitate the Protestant Church to which "the ministry of the word" is so central. True, scholars like Leopold Zunz, the giant of the nineteenth century "Science of Judaism" could prove that the sermon is an integral part of Jewish tradition. But the need to deploy scholarship came from the desire to make the synagogue, or at least the temple, correspond to the norms of the dominant religion. That desire has now gone. Jewish worshippers, even ardent liberals, feel no need to refer and defer to Christian practices. The current norms are not shaped by the churches but by secular institutions — civil religion again.

And in these institutions the lecture and the sermon have been replaced by the moving picture and slide presentation. The 30-second segment has to tell it all. Television, not the live, spoken word, is the conveyor of truth in our time; even newspapers, unless they are tabloids, are suffering. People avoid potentially interesting lectures to watch a television programme at home. The sermon is seen as old-fashioned in content and form and, therefore, cannot be taken seriously. It is a relic from a distant past that stirs negative feelings — envy, hostility — and reflects outdated techniques. Judaism knows, of course, that when the image replaces the word, idolatry has triumphed. But many Jews don't realize it or don't care.

Franz Rosenzweig, the most influential Jewish thinker of this century, had personally experienced the power of the sermon. He wrote in a letter to a friend, following the High Holy Day Services in 1921, in praise of Rabbi Nehemiah Nobel of Frankfurt:

> Nobel's sermons were incredibly magnificent. Nothing would be too audacious for him to risk saying at such moments, and there is nothing that would not be true coming from such a mouth. Think of this happening to me, who hates and detests all sermons . . . He prays the way one thinks of people praying only thousands of years ago, when the great prayers originated. He speaks to the

people as one thinks only the prophets should have been allowed to speak.[3]

Rosenzweig knew the power of the word and its centrality in Judaism. Our ancestors were not given 10 commandments at Sinai, but 10 words, *dibrot*. One word forbids us to make visual images lest they become idols, but we are bidden to speak and listen. The mouth — "O Lord, open my lips that my mouth shall declare Your praise" — and the ear — "Hear, O Israel" — are the most important parts of the Jewish body. To give in to the fashions of our time, and the prejudices of our people, may be tantamount to betraying our heritage.

The form of the sermon may need changing, but its place remains central. More Jews are exposed to sermons than to books or journals where ideas are being presented. Even if rabbis are not the originators of these ideas, they are readers of books and journals. Often they disseminate the ideas, even if selectively and sermonically, to their congregations. The likelihood is, therefore, that anything that is new will often be heard from the pulpit, often from different perspectives in different contexts.

Halachah, 'Jewish law,' has to be precise and unequivocal. But the spoken word can, and must, be open to more than one interpretation to reflect *divrey elohim chayim,* 'the words of the living God,' and thus have the power to stir mind and heart. That is why *aggada,* that is, all that is not *halachah* in rabbinic tradition, is the stuff of which sermons have been crafted. The riches of aggadic *midrash,* the stories and homilies of rabbis, and *chasidic* tales and modern interpretations, all find their way into the contemporary sermon in its endeavour to inform and to stir the modern Jew. The pulpit is an open forum for much of what is current and significant in contemporary Jewish thought. The sermons seek to build bridges between the tradition that beckons us and the reality that bedevils us. The preacher tries to make the connection between past and present.

That is why the sermon, at times, goes beyond the classical sources and creates interpretations of its own. A fellow student in my homiletics class at Leo Baeck College in London once criticized our teacher, the late Ignaz Maybaum, for not using enough *midrash* in his sermons. "True," said Maybaum, "I don't quote much *midrash;* I make it." The gifted preacher creates *midrash* by bringing the text to the people, even when the congregation purports to be asleep.

Yet another dimension of the modern sermon must be mentioned in this context. The rabbi is often the only believing Jew whom many people encounter. It is an education to understand how such a Jew thinks and what he or she feels. For many, it has been a revelation to discover you can be as educated and intelligent as the next person and yet believe, without setting aside your secular knowledge or compromising your intelligence. That is why, not only *what* is being said from the pulpit is important, but *how* it is being said and *who* is saying it. Dedicated preachers reveal not only their minds, but their souls.

The effect, therefore, is often greater than the congregation is prepared to admit. In more than 30 years of committed preaching, I have observed how many men and women have assimilated the ideas they heard from the pulpit, making them their own, despite initial indifference or even opposition. The word of God is more powerful than the human ear, and persistent enough to penetrate even a closed mind. That is why preaching is so important, even when it appears to be unpopular. That is also why rabbis must persevere and curb their sarcasm and sense of despondency. If the prophets could withstand the hostility of their contemporaries, modern rabbis can learn to live with their frustrations.

Rabbi Haskel Lookstein's words of introduction to the volume of sermons that he and his colleagues of the New York Board of Rabbis published reflect much truth, although they sound self-serving to sceptics: "A sermon is designed to elicit response. It must do more than inform; it must also inspire. It must enlighten our minds; but it should also ennoble our behaviour. It should teach our congregants in the areas which we know best; but it should also stimulate our listeners to be better Jews and human beings."[4]

Many contemporary sermons do precisely that. Worshippers would, of course, benefit much more by paying attention rather than being only subliminally affected. Some are taking notice and actually enjoying sermons more than collecting for the building fund. They may encourage others, so "the stone which the builders rejected" may again "become the chief cornerstone" (Psalms 118:22), of the synagogue, and the empty prayer palaces can be filled with Torah and worship.

Notes

1 Jonathan S. Woocher, *Sacred Survival: The Civil Religion of American Jews* (Bloomington & Indianapolis: Indiana University Press, 1986), 16.

2 Ibid., 17.

3 Quoted in Nahum N. Glatzer, *Franz Rosenzweig: His Life and Thought* (New York: Schocken, 1961), 103–4.

4 Saul I. Teplitz (editor), *The Rabbis Speak* (New York: The New York Board of Rabbis, 1986), xiii.

25

Being Alone with God

In *The School of Genius,* Anthony Storr challenges a view articulated by psychotherapists and social workers, and reflected in Martin Buber's philosophy, that the essence of human existence is relationship, particularly relating to other human beings.[1] Storr, an eminent British psychiatrist, disagrees with Buber that all reality is meeting. Yes, relationships are important, but so is solitude; a balanced person has both.

Storr quotes the famous British child psychiatrist Donald Winnicott. Winnicott "suggests that the capacity to be alone, first in the presence of the mother, and then in her absence, is also related to the individual's capacity to get in touch with, and make manifest, his own true feelings."

Storr understands this to mean that "it is only when the child has experienced a contented, relaxed sense of being alone with, and then without, the mother, that he can be sure of being able to discover what he really needs or wants, irrespective of what others may expect or try to foist upon him." This ability to be alone without fear lays the groundwork for a true liberal, someone who can make informed choices (a favourite Reform cliché). All this leads Storr to conclude: "The capacity to be alone thus becomes linked with self-discovery and self-realization; with becoming aware of one's deepest needs, feelings, and impulses."[2]

Statement presented at a meeting of the Commission on Religious Living of the Union of American Hebrew Congregations, Atlanta, Georgia, November 20, 1988.

Even my oblique reference to Reform Judaism above, does not justify my references to psychoanalytic theory as suitable material for a statement at this meeting. Let me, therefore, try to redeem myself by quoting another passage from Storr's book.

> Another analogy to Winnicott's concept of the capacity to be alone is prayer. Prayer goes far beyond merely asking for benefits for oneself or for others. Prayer can be a public act of worship; but the person who prays in private feels himself to be alone in the presence of God. This is another way of putting the individual in touch with his deepest feelings. In some religions, no response to prayer from any supernatural being is even expected. Prayer is undertaken, not with the intention of influencing a deity, nor with any hope of prayers being directly answered, but in order to produce a harmonious state of mind. Prayer and meditation facilitate integration by allowing time for previously unrelated thoughts and feelings to interact.[3]

There is, of course, much more to Jewish prayer than is implied in Storr's description. But there can never be less. It was never less with, for example, the biblical characters who prayed. For one dimension of prayer is always being alone in the presence of God. A congregation, a sanctuary, a familiar setting often make it easier — paradoxically — to be alone before God. Interacting with other like-minded men and women at services is the other relational dimension of worship.

Praying in *shul* is like playing in the park with other children, watched over by a loving parent yet also allowed to be on one's own, to find oneself as a person. And like such play, prayer is a way of growing up. To the extent that a child can be alone with a parent, he or she can also face the world without parents. To the extent that we know how to be alone in the presence of God, we will learn to cope with the world when God seems absent, hidden.

Thinking of prayer in terms of Storr's psychological reflections raises several important issues. First, psychological insights are helpful in our endeavours to come to terms with this most vexing issue for moderns:

how to pray. But such insights confuse us if we turn services into group therapy, letting religion imitate psychotherapy rather than learning from and integrating psychotherapy into the religious life.

Second, our existing liturgies with their rigid structures — telling us when to sit and when to stand, and even which prayers to read aloud — turn praying individuals into a silent, or at best, mumbling mass. They rarely help a person be alone in the presence of God.

Third, I have always tried to persuade people that you need not solve all your theological problems before you start praying. Praying reflects a need, a yearning for wholeness in a disjointed world and a disjointed self. It is not a statement of certainty; the grammatical forms of many Hebrew prayers are much more tentative than the English translations suggest. Storr's insights offer new arguments in my endeavour to make this point.

Fourth, many sensitive men and women turn away from our Reform synagogues to go elsewhere — sometimes to other synagogues, often to cults — in search of an ambiance that will allow them to be alone in the presence of God among like-minded people. They are in search of an experience of the holy, but find in our circles very little beyond disciplined conviviality. They yearn for growth before God to discover meaning in their lives, but feel their needs are not met.

I would not find it difficult to draw some practical conclusions from these observations, but that is not within my brief. All I know is that if A. N. Whitehead, the British philosopher, is right in defining religion as that which a person does with his or her solitariness, then Storr's understanding of prayer becomes one way we can all express religiosity. It does not cover all aspects of Judaism, or even of prayer, but it seems to point to one that is often neglected in our liberal, collectivist way of organizing religious services.

Notes

1 Anthony Storr, *The School of Genius* (London: Andre Deutsch, 1988).

2 Ibid., 21.

3 Ibid., 28.

Index